Where Angels Dwell

Where Angels Dwell

EDITED AND COMPLILED BY
DORSEY L. BURK

Copyright 2000
Foreign Missions Division
United Pentecostal Church International
8855 Dunn Road
Hazelwood, MO 63042

Contents

1. Botswana: Saved from an Angry Mob — 9
by Rick Perry
2. Burkina Faso: Teach Us to Pray — 13
by Craig Sully
3. Cameroon: From a Volkswagen to a — 15
Motor Home by Angie Fackler
4. Ghana: You Just Never Know — 19
by James Poitras
5. Kenya: He Changed My Direction — 23
by Jimmy Hall
6. Uganda: Early Morning Call — 27
by Darline Kantola Royer
7. Japan: Jesse's Miracles — 33
by Richard Lucas
8. Korea: Kaleidoscope of Korea — 37
by Elton Bernard
9. Nepal: A Hindu Finds Christ — 43
submitted by Stanley Scism
10. Dominican Republic: Brother Agustin's Shack — 47
by Jerry Burns
11. El Salvador: God Is Our Protector — 49
by Bruce A. Howell
12. El Salvador: The Van That Flew — 55
by Bruce A. Howell
13. El Salvador: Lesson in Humility — 57
by Scotty Slaydon
14. Guyana: God Sent It—Let's Grab It! — 61
by Janeace Miller
15. Guyana: The Miraculous Blackout — 65
by Loren D. Miller
16. Jamaica: The Revival in Golden Grove — 67
by Rachel Smith

17.	Belgium: Lydia's Story by Brenda Ciulla	73
18.	Eastern Europe: Where Angels Dwell by Samuel Balca	77
19.	The Netherlands: He Sent His Word and Healed by Michael Tuttle	81
20.	United Kingdom: Doing the Kangaroo Hop by Mervyn D. Miller	85
21.	Guam: Twenty-one Nations Hear the Gospel by Monte Showalter	89
22.	Hawaii: Thankful by Sue Robertson	95
23.	Papua New Guinea: Japheth's Miracle by Esther Henry	99
24.	Philippines: He Is More Than Enough for Me! submitted by David Brott	103
25.	Philippines: As He Said, "Jesus!" by Cecil Sullivan	107
26.	Singapore: Sister Jocelyn and Silkair Flight MI 185 by Steve Willoughby	111
27.	Argentina: I Still Know the Peace Speaker by Kay Burgess	115
28.	Chile: The Accident That Did Not Happen by Roy Well	121
29.	Ecuador: Sacrificial Giving by Stuart Lassetter	123
30.	Faith Promise Ministries: It Really Does Work! submitted by Mervyn D. Miller	125

Preface

Listening to missionaries tell their stories, as they stopped by my home church, kindled my interest in missions. To my young mind, their stories were exciting, challenging, uplifting, and convicting. They increased my faith in a God who would provide and protect and made me want to dedicate my life to Him and to be used by Him. Those storytellers stood out to me as giants of faith, devotion, and sacrifice.

A new generation of missionaries has taken the place of those I listened to as a child. However, they too stand out to me as spiritual giants—men and women who are willing to answer the call of God, go wherever He leads, and trust Him to supply their needs. And their stories are just as inspiring.

Where Angels Dwell is the second volume of missionary stories produced by Foreign Missions Division. These stories, written by United Pentecostal Church International missionaries, both past and present, will challenge, amuse, thrill, and uplift you. You will gain insight to missionary life as you share the missionaries' struggles and triumphs. Your faith will grow as you read about miracles of divine supply and protection.

Because you asked for more, *Where Angels Dwell* invites you to soar into the heavenlies.

—Dorsey L. Burk

Chapter 1

Botswana: Saved from an Angry Mob

By **Rick Perry**
Associate in missions to Botswana

In a village approximately twenty miles from Botswana's capital city of Gaborone, a businessman and his partners sought the advice of a local witch doctor about how they could prosper in business. The witch doctor instructed the man to kill his little daughter as a sacrifice for success in the business world. Inconceivably, the man and his partners followed the witch doctor's advice and sacrificed his daughter on the altar of materialism.

Naturally, this was not something that the authorities could overlook. They arrested the men after finding the girl's body parts in the father's refrigerator. After going to court, the men were released, however. Meanwhile, University of Botswana students became upset and began to protest, demanding justice.

My wife and I were at a shopping center where I was getting a haircut. We then indulged ourselves with some good African cooking at a restaurant in the shopping center. While we were eating, people began rushing into the restaurant, asking to use the phone, while other shopkeepers were locking their doors and putting "Closed" signs in the windows.

We asked what was going on and learned that students were rioting in the main mall, a section of our downtown area, and that they were headed our way. We cut our meal short and headed for the car to get away from the situation. Unfortunately, we were a bit too late as the riot had already spread to our location. Military police and helicopters were everywhere, but they were not enough for the thousands of protesters. Several policemen escorted us to our truck, and we drove to the home of my brother-in-law, Brian Williams. (Brian and Lakelie Williams were associates in missions to Botswana at that time but are now missionaries to Kazakhstan.)

When people riot, the police can rarely maintain order. Frequently it evolves into a more complicated situation than just demonstrating, and people take their anger out on the innocent. After several hours Brian and I took the vehicle out to see if things had calmed down. After all, we had seen vehicles burning and people lying in the roads, beaten and bloody. You can only imagine the fright of the situation.

We turned down a main road and went around a corner only to see a mob numbering five hundred people or more coming straight at us. I then turned the vehicle around to head in the other direction. However, another group had gathered from that side as well. We were left with no option other than to drive straight toward them at a high speed, hoping they would move. If we would have sat still, I don't know if I would be able to tell this story. So we put the "pedal to the metal" and headed toward them.

They began throwing stones, rocks, and boulders until no windows were left in the vehicle. The vehicle looked like it had been in a major accident, and we looked like the survivors of that accident! With glass all in our arms and other parts of our body, we went back to the Williamses' home and locked the gates and doors for several more hours until it was safe to leave. We thank God for saving us from the mob on that day!

Rick Perry arrived in Botswana as an associate in missions in August 1993. As the months passed, he fell in love with the work and with Stacey Simoneaux, who went to Botswana as an AIMer in 1992 to help her parents, Rev. and Mrs. Tim Simoneaux. The were married in August 1994.

Brother Perry stated, "Upon my arrival I worked with The Learning Centre School, which at the time had about twenty-six students. I was the grass cutter, bus driver, and many more things. The school is now running roughly 600 students. I serve as the assistant school director, and my wife serves as the director of our pre-school.

"In addition to working in the Christian school, we have started a church and taught many Bible studies. My wife is also heavily involved in ladies ministry while I work with the the youth. I serve as the vice president of Streams in the Desert Ministries, which operates a resource center, and Bible training courses for our local church. In the future it will also include such things as an orphanage for orphaned AIDS children."

Chapter 2

Burkina Faso: Teach Us to Pray

By **Craig Sully**
Missionary to Burkina Faso

Teaching our kids about prayer can be difficult sometimes. One night during our bedtime prayers, Jeffrey prayed for "sunshine." After we were all done, I explained that we were in the dry season, and it is sunny every day. It was like praying for air to breathe. It would happen whether you prayed for it or not. I further encouraged him to see for himself that God does answer prayer by asking for something "hard," like rain in the dry season, for instance. As it is not supposed to rain in Burkina Faso until April or May, that would be a miracle.

A few days later at breakfast, he told me, "Dad, if you want to see how powerful God is, ask for snow and ice!" I explained that asking for that would be bad as people would get sick and maybe die since they are not used to the cold. Still I wanted him to know that God does answer prayer.

After running around much of the day, I came home that afternoon to some pretty excited people. Just a few minutes earlier it had hailed at our house. Apparently this happens occasionally in the middle of the rainy season. However, the African woman who was at our house at the time said that she had never seen it happen during the dry season. In fact the two men who came home with me for a meeting simply did not believe that it had happened. I must admit that I had noticed some dark clouds and thought that it would be quite neat if it did rain, though I am not sure I had the faith to make it happen. Needless to say, this was a great lesson in the power of prayer.

In 1987 Craig Sully, a graduate of United Pentecostal Bible Institute, Fredericton, New Brunswick, began his foreign missions involvement by serving as an associate in missions in Nigeria. The following year, Lyna Paramore arrived in Nigeria to fulfill the call of God upon her life. They later married and returned to Nigeria to continue serving as associates in missions. In 1991 the Sullys received their missionary appointment to Nigeria. They taught in the Bible school, trained ministers, and evangelized.

In 1996 the Foreign Missions Board granted the Sullys' request to transfer to Ivory Coast. The Sullys completed their French language study at the Missions Language Training Center in Albertsville, France, in June 1998. In January 1999 the Foreign Missions Board changed the Sullys' appointment to Burkina Faso so that they could lead and nurture the young church there. They arrived in their new field in September 1999.

Chapter 3

Cameroon: From a Volkswagen to a Motor Home

By **Angie Fackler**
Missionary to Cameroon

Just before my husband and I married, he took an old Volkswagen that belonged to one of the missionaries and fixed it up. He did this so that we would have a car when we returned to Nigeria as associates in missions after our wedding in Louisiana. It took every extra penny we had to keep it running, but it got us to where we were going for the first two years that we were married. We were thankful for it. When it came time for us to return to the United States for a short furlough, our superintendent, Missionary Johnny Garrison, asked if we would be willing to give the Volkswagen to the national leader. After we agreed to do so, Brother Garrison told us that God would bless us with the money for a better vehicle while we were home.

"Well, suppose we get the money for a vehicle while home," I asked him just before leaving Nigeria, "how much would it cost for us to buy a decent car here?"

"Five thousand dollars would buy you a pretty nice car with air conditioning," he answered.

Just a few days after we arrived home, our friends, Mark and Ginger Majors, called from Melville,

Louisiana. "We know you're just getting home, but as soon as you can, why don't you come by to see us. We have something to tell you." So a few days later, while we were sitting in their office, Mark began to explain to us that God had been blessing their transportation business. They had told the Lord that for every increase, they would give a certain percentage to missions.

"We knew you were coming home," he said, "so we've been saving this for you and your work. I don't really know what your needs are, but if you need a vehicle, we would really like for the money to go toward helping you with that. But you are free to use the money for whatever you need it for. It's up to you." My husband and I did not say a word but let them finish with what they had to say. Then Ginger said, "We are glad to present you with five thousand dollars."

We then began to explain what had taken place the week before; we all realized that God had orchestrated it all. So, when we returned to Nigeria two months later, we were able to buy a nice car. And it even had air conditioning—what a luxury!

After being in Nigeria for another year, we got a call from Brother and Sister Terry Riddick, missionaries to Cameroon, asking us to come there to serve as their furlough replacements. Due to the extremely high toll on vehicles brought into Cameroon, we were unable to take the car and were not quite sure what to do with it.

Some weeks later, I was praying and felt strongly impressed that we should give the car to Brother and Sister Jim Poitras, missionaries in Nigeria. I walked into the house and said to my husband, "Allan, I need to tell you something."

"Let me tell you something first," he said. "I don't know how you're going to feel about this, but I think we need to give our car to the Poitrases. Brother Poitras

Cameroon: From a Volkswagen to a Motor Home

travels out to visit our churches almost every weekend, and Sister Poitras is left at home with those two small babies. If she were to have an emergency, I don't know what she would do. I know the car would be a blessing to them."

"That's what I was going to tell you," I said. So it was agreed; we gave the car to the Poitrases, and they fondly referred to it as "The Blessing."

Then there was the question of what we were going to drive while in Cameroon. It just so happened that after we decided to give the car to the Poitras family, we received permission to use the Riddicks' vehicle during our time as their furlough replacements. God had provided another vehicle!

It seems that from that time on, everywhere we went God always provided us a vehicle. At every new place, we had something to drive.

At our deputation orientation, we were talking to Brother John Leaman about our travel plans. "What are you planning to travel in?" he asked. "It sure would be nice if you could get a motor home with those two babies."

"Well, Brother Leaman," I said, "God has always provided a vehicle for us. I'm going to believe Him for a motor home."

"Well," he replied with a chuckle, "God can certainly do it."

Just three weeks before we were scheduled to begin deputational travel, our former pastor, Brother Ray Majors from Melville, Louisiana, invited us to be in service with him for the weekend. While we were there, he told us that he had a motor home that we could use for our deputation. He didn't want us to buy it or to even lease it, but he was giving it to us to use for our entire deputation. All we had to do was pick it up and

17

drop it off in his yard when we were done with it. About a month later, I saw Brother Leaman again at a conference. "Well, Brother Leaman, God provided a motor home for our deputation."

"Yeah, I heard about that. Isn't that something!"

It sure was something! But really, I expected Him to do it. He had always done it before. I didn't figure He was about to change!

Angie Fackler met her husband, Allan, while they both were serving as associates in missions in Nigeria and Cameroon respectively. Together they have served in Nigeria, Cameroon, Kenya, and Curacao. In 1995 they helped found the Bible school in Cameroon and served as administrator, nurse, and instructors. Brother Fackler holds a secondary education teacher's certificate and is a licensed practical nurse, while his wife has a bachelor's degree in behavioral sciences. Their immediate desire is to continue in these capacities, with future plans of training nationals to continue the work.

The Facklers received their missionary appointment to Cameroon in October 1998 and departed for the field in late December 1999.

Chapter 4

Ghana: You Just Never Know!

By **Jim Poitras**
Missionary to Ghana

Have you ever wondered what could be the result of your individual witness on the job, school, or in any other sector of life?

In 1979 I was pursuing a bachelor of education degree at the University of New Brunswick. I was doing my best to live for God according to what I knew and did not know, being raised in the Roman Catholic Church. While looking through the local newspaper, friends noticed an advertisement for the local United Pentecostal Church. I knew nothing about the UPCI but strongly stated, nonetheless, "It will be over my dead body that I ever walk through the doors of that church."

To help pay for my education I worked at the local Metropolitan Department Store. On staff was a high school student named Lynne. There was something very special and attractive about her. I just couldn't put my finger on what set her apart from all the other people who worked in the store and went to my school. One Saturday night, I asked her out on a date.

She quickly enlightened me that this would not be possible. She also told me that she was attending a revival at her local church. Well, I had been used to church and did not think that there would be any harm in that, so I invited myself to go along. What a surprise! The Pentecostal service was a shocking experience compared to where I went to church. I was not familiar with the loud praying, the various forms of demonstrative worship, the screaming choir, or the screeching preaching. Then there was the altar call. I had been down to the altar before and signed my name on dotted lines, accepting the Lord as my personal Savior. Each time, I had left the altar the same way that I had gone to it—a sinner.

This time was different, however. There was no card to sign, and I quickly exhausted all the words I knew how to pray. Then someone introduced me to Acts 2:38. I had not even known that there was a Book of Acts. This trip to the altar was different. It really should be referred to as an alter and not an altar, because it altered my life. I was never the same. I left different that night, thanks to the power of God, the preaching of the gospel, and the witness of Lynne.

Some thought I would never stay. My parents demanded that I not stay if I wanted to remain a part of the family. They had heard of "Holy Rollers" before. However, my mind was made up and my life changed. I never have looked back and do not plan to give up now. I graduated from the university and immediately went to Nigeria as an associate in missions. I had only been in the church for three years. Now the gospel seed, planted in my life by a teenager named Lynne, was not only bearing fruit but also reproducing itself on foreign soil.

My wife and I received our missionary appointment in 1985 and have served as missionaries in two West African nations. Now the Lord has allowed me to serve Him as superintendent of a growing, thriving national church organization in Ghana and as the area coordinator of six English-speaking nations in West Africa. During the past sixteen years on the mission field, we have trained hundreds of men and women to reach their world with the truth of God's Word. In the last three and one-half years, 6,515 people have received the Holy Ghost in Ghana alone. You just never know what God will do through someone you witness to.

I should also tell you about what happened to Lynne. She, too, went to the mission field. Her full name is Lynne Jewett. She gave up everything she had and served under the Wynn Drost family in Guatemala and Mexico. After many years under the AIM program, she was appointed as a missionary and is giving herself to the training of others in Guatemala. She is working with Brad Thompson, whose family was responsible for keeping me in the church after Lynne brought me there that first Sunday night.

You just never know! Through your individual witness, you may be the key to world evangelism. You can impact this world, not only through your prayers and finances, but also with your life. As one man preached, "The Human Touch for the Human Race!"

Jim and Linda Poitras, both professional educators, met in Nigeria as associates in missions, married, and later received their missionary appointment in 1985. Following more than a decade in Nigeria, they accepted the challenge to go to Ghana, lead the work, and restore the inactive training program there.

Arriving in Ghana in February 1995, Brother Poitras became the field superintendent. He opened ACTS-Ghana and built a beautiful Bible school facility. He wrote *Acts: God's Training Manual for Today's Church,* which is the curriculum for Portable Bible Schools. In January 1996 he became the area coordinator of the English-speaking nations of West Africa. He also serves as the chairman of the Africa Aflame Committee, whose vision is to provide material and implement guidelines for leadership development, literature, and training.

Linda Poitras remains active by serving as the national ladies president, an instructor at ACTS-Ghana, and their daughters' teacher.

The Poitrases returned to the field in early 2000.

Chapter 5

Kenya: He Changed My Direction

By **Jimmy Hall**
Missionary to Kenya, Burundi, Rwanda

Around 10:15 AM on Friday, August 7, 1998, I was driving into Nairobi with two American guests to do some shopping before they left the next morning. The shop that we had wanted to visit was near the American Embassy. As we entered the main part of town, I felt impressed that we should wait until the afternoon to go in that direction, so we ended up in the main city market. Within a short time, I recognized that people were tense and very nervous. Not wanting to alarm my guests, I quickly parked and asked some shop owners about the apparent problem. They told us of the bomb blast in town that had just taken place. A large bomb had exploded at the American Embassy during the time that I had decided change our direction. Even then, I had no idea of the seriousness of this tragedy.

When we reached home, my wife, Pat, was so relieved that we were okay. She had heard the news of how extensive the explosion was and knew that we were going to that part of town. The telephone rang constantly from friends and acquaintances wanting to know if we were safe. I have thanked the Lord many times since then for changing my direction. Much damage occurred on the street where we were headed, and the glass windows that shattered and flew in all directions injured many people.

Roberta, an American woman who works at the embassy and attends our church, would have normally been at work that day. However, one of her children needed medical attention, so they had left Nairobi for the United States on the Saturday before the bomb went off. Her boss was killed and her coworkers were injured. She would have more than likely been one of the causalities as well.

Roberta's husband was on the fourth floor when the bomb exploded. The floor above him collapsed all around him, encasing him in a concrete box that he rode to the ground floor. He walked out of the building shaken up but unharmed. We believe that God saved this family because of the prayers going up for them.

Sister Oyoko, a Nairobi pastor's wife, works a couple of buildings away from the American Embassy. She was on the fourteenth floor, where large glass windows form the outer wall. Just moments before the explosion, something impressed her to step into another room without windows. She was not hurt at all, while other workers suffered cuts and injuries from flying glass.

A man in their church was traveling in a minivan close to the embassy with other morning passengers. He said he heard the explosion, and the next thing he remembers is being in the hospital. He had just a few scratches; everyone else in the van was killed.

We have sixteen UPCI churches in Nairobi, and we had no reports of any our people injured or killed. We give God all the praise and glory for protecting His people. Truly this was a great miracle, seeing that the bomb went off where so many people travel in and out of the city. We heard testimonies of those who were in the area and left early, of those who were impressed to take a different route, and of others who called in to take off work that day.

As of August 18, 1998, over 257 people were dead, 4,000 were injured, and many others were still hospitalized. Twelve Americans and thirty Kenyan staff members at the American Embassy lost their lives. Over half of the 200 people who worked at the American Embassy were killed or injured. We wept with America as well as with the country of Kenya.

We received messages from many of our churches, pastors, friends, family, and fellow missionaries. Several told us that God had impressed them to pray for us that week. We give God the glory for His protection and thank everyone for his or her prayers.

In May 1979 Jimmy Hall, the Kansas District secretary, and his wife, Pat, were appointed as UPCI missionaries to Liberia. In Liberia Brother Hall served as the field superintendent, overseeing the growth and outreach of the UPC of Liberia, and as the president of Maranatha Bible School in Monrovia.

In 1991 the Foreign Missions Board asked the Halls to assume the field superintendence of Kenya. In this position Brother Hall is the chief administrative officer of the UPC of Kenya. He also teaches at Life Tabernacle Bible School in Nairobi and oversees the development of the United Pentecostal Church in neighboring Rwanda and Burundi.

Sister Hall is active in ladies ministries and also teaches in the Bible school.

Chapter 6

Uganda: Early Morning Call

By **Darline Kantola Royer**
Missionary to Uganda

Soon after the sun rose above the eastern hill, the ringing telephone stirred us from our slumber. Early morning calls usually awaken a sense of fearful concern, as did this one. I heard my husband, Arlon, say, "Oh, I'm sorry to hear that. When did it happen?" Not hearing the other end of the conversation, I felt that sting of fear. Who? What? Where? I knew from the sound of Arlon's voice that he had been given tragic news. Was it from family or friends in the USA? Was it one of our preachers? Was it someone's child? When I heard him say, "We'll be there right away," I knew that some of our dear people here in Kampala had faced tragedy.

As Arlon hung up the phone, he reported, "Mama Tunda just passed away." Mama Tunda, the mother of two of our preachers in Kampala, had been such a strength and support to her two preacher sons, as well as a faithful, industrious wife to her husband, Brother Tunda.

Mama Tunda received the Holy Ghost several years ago when her family accepted the Apostolic message in Rwanda, but for many years she rejected the necessity of baptism in Jesus' name. The genocidal devastation in

Rwanda in 1994 resulted in this family's settling in Kampala. Then in September 1999, we had the joyful experience of watching Mama Tunda's eldest son baptize her in Jesus' name after Brother Ron Garrett from Glendale, Arizona, preached a convicting message about the necessity of being baptized in the name of Jesus.

Her recent burial in the name of Jesus took the sting out of her burial this late afternoon. As we spent much of our day with the family, we witnessed their intense expression of grief. We watched their tears flow; we heard their anguished cries of "Mama yangu, mama yangu, umeacha mimi!" (My mother, my mother, you have left me!) "Umeenda wapi?" (You have gone where?) We sorrowed with her precious husband as he sat silenced by lonely grief.

Yes, we wept with them, stood by them, and sat near them while they grieved. As is their custom, their deceased mother lay on a foam mattress on the floor of their humble home, awaiting the visit of family, friends, and neighbors throughout the morning and afternoon.

In the midst of the sorrowing, the elder son, Pastor Reny, assumed his expected family role and set about to make the hurried funeral arrangements. Without the benefit of embalming, in the tropical weather the burial needed to be done before nightfall. As we drove back home to fax a message to the two sons and one daughter living in eastern Congo, we dropped Pastor Reny off in town to arrange for a burial plot. When we returned a short time later to the home, they had placed her body in a wooden casket and had made plans for a 4:00 PM devotion in their home prior to the burial. At the family's request, we rushed home again to get our camera and to be on hand for Arlon to read some Scripture and to offer some words of comfort.

As husband, sons, daughter, and four grandchildren

stood beside Mama Tunda's casket, Arlon, flanked by other relatives and friends, shared the comfort of God's Word with them and prayed for them. Then we stood silent as we waited for the vehicles to come to transport the casket, family members, and friends to the burial place.

As the casket was placed in the bed of a pickup, the family members climbed in beside it for the farewell ride with their loved one. Our Sheaves for Christ Nissan and two other vans followed behind on a ten-minute ride, which led us along winding, pothole filled streets and down several dirt lanes to the burial site. Because most Ugandans are buried on family plots in country areas, cemeteries are neither common nor well kept. Such was this one!

On arrival at the site, several men carted the casket to the prepared grave and immediately began lowering it to its final resting place. As the mourners circled the grave, sounds of grief pierced the stillness of the late afternoon. A few jumped down into the grave to pull back the white sheet from the protective glass in order to glimpse the face of their departed loved one for one last time. As they had requested, Arlon stepped to the foot of the grave, opened his Bible, and again shared with them God's Word, imparting to them the counsel of the Lord in times of sorrow and loss and closing his comments with prayer.

After the prayer, a man lifted a shovel full of dirt in front of Arlon, indicating that he should toss the first handful of dirt into the grave. Then others followed, each tossing in his handful of dirt. With that custom complete, the mourners burst forth into songs of praise to the Lord, while different men took turns shoveling the dirt into the grave. Grief turned into joy, acknowledging that a saint had gone to her reward.

When the grave was covered and the dirt neatly spread, the younger son, who had been overcome with grief, stepped up and began to join the men in cleaning the weeds and grass from the grave to leave it attractively groomed. As they finished, they handed Arlon a rustic wooden cross, which he placed as the grave headstone before offering the final prayer. The graveside service closed with the reading of the obituary and comments from a family member.

The funeral caravan then returned to the family home to eat a meal of sweet potatoes and beans. During this time, the immediate family sat together on the floor of the empty living room where the casket had lain. Friends continued trickling in to offer their condolences, having received the word later in the day. After the sun had set behind the horizon, the family asked Arlon to preach God's Word to them and to all who lingered there.

Once again he opened his Bible and offered strength and comfort from God's Word. Sitting on the sidelines, I found reason to rejoice in watching grief-stricken family members rise from their morning hours of deep despair to evening moments of peace and rest in God's love.

As we said our farewells to them, preparing to return home, a father and his two sons gripped our hands with confidence, which testified that they had found comfort in the Lord. The daughter, who had been so gripped with grief throughout the day, lay peacefully resting. Yes, complications of malaria and diabetes had brought the sting of death to their home, but they found the victory of faith. God gave them comfort! And we give God praise!

Yes, we do!

Arlon and Darline Royer's thirty years of pastoral and teaching ministry in the United States, seasoned with a missionary ministry in Kenya, provided experience and insight for laying the foundation of the United Apostolic Church of Uganda. Stepping into a country that was recuperating from more than two decades of civil, economic, and spiritual devastation, the Royers faced a great challenge.

Soon after registering the church, the Royers launched into Mobile Bible School ministries (two-week programs involving sixty hours of study) and extensive travel to strengthen and encourage village pastors and to promote church growth. To enhance training and evangelism, the Royers printed eighteen books plus over 450,000 copies of tracts. They also distributed hand-cranked tape players for bilingual cassette tapes and built portable tent-frame buildings for MBS accommodations.

In June 1998 the Royers opened a new church in Kampala to serve as a model and outreach to the nation.

The Royers went on furlough in January 1999.

Chapter 7

Japan: Jesse's Miracles

By **Richard Lucas**
Missionary to Japan

In the fall of 1997 one of the Ghanaian families in our church in Tokyo, the Gyamfis, noticed that their eighteen-month-old son, Jesse, was dragging his leg as he walked. When they took him to the hospital for tests, the doctor told them—and showed them on the X-ray—that Jesse's leg was out of the socket and that the muscle in his hip was damaged. He said it would require major surgery and referred them to a specialist who would be able to perform it.

The Gyamfis brought the child to the house of God, and we prayed for Jesse at the beginning of the service. During the song service the little boy slipped away from his parents and stepped out into the aisle. Clapping his hands and leaping in perfect time to the music, Jesse made his way to right in front of the pulpit. Without looking around at others, he stayed right in front of the pulpit, clapping, raising his hands, and sincerely worshiping.

His dad came and took him back to the seat, and the boy began to cry. We ask parents not to let their children run around. However, this was so unusual that I went to the dad and told him that if the boy wanted to worship, please not to stop him. I had never seen such a small boy do anything like that before and could not help wondering if the Lord was doing something special for him. As soon as Brother Gyamfi let him go, the little fellow came right back up front and resumed his joyous, intent worship.

That week the parents took the child to the specialist. After he had taken more X-rays and tests, the specialist became angry. He said, "There is something wrong. The doctor who sent you to me has made some kind of mix-up or something." He showed them the X-rays of Jesse's leg sent by the other doctor and the X-ray he had just taken. He said, "You can see here the severe problem on this X-ray [the first one], but on the X-rays and tests we took today there is no problem with your son's leg at all. It is perfect." They told him about the prayer. He said, "Well, your son's leg is absolutely perfect now."

When the child's father came out from talking to the doctor, he found his wife surrounded by some of the Japanese nurses who knew their case. She was telling them what the Lord had done, and some of them were openly weeping. One Japanese lady, with tears flowing down her cheeks, said, "If God could do this for your son, then maybe He would help my daughter. If I may, I want to bring her to your church and have her prayed for."

I was preparing an article on Jesse's miracle when I received a call that he had been rushed to the hospital in a coma. He was in very severe, continuous convulsions. He had an extremely high temperature and acute swelling of his brain. He also had a critically high amount of two different types of infection raging in his body. The doctors briefed the parents and told them that there was little hope that Jesse could live. If he did live, it was doubtful he would ever come out of the coma. Almost certainly he had little hope of ever walking or speaking again.

When I arrived at the hospital, we had prayer, and the Lord touched Jesse. The convulsions immediately stopped. Over the following days, prayer continued, and as it did, the Lord continued to do things in Jesse that amazed the doctors. The swelling of the brain went down, the fever dropped, and Jesse came out of the coma. His improvement continued steadily over the following weeks.

The Gyamfis brought Jesse back to church on the first Sunday after his release from the hospital. We prayed, and on that day Jesse began walking again. A few weeks later during worship service, Jesse again slipped off his dad's lap and came down to the front, clapping his hands and leaping in time to the music again.

Since then the Japanese lady to whom the Gyamfis witnessed has come to church with her husband and two daughters. The Lord has dramatically touched her daughter. She and her husband have received the Holy Ghost. Her husband was baptized, and she was later baptized on Easter Sunday, 1998.

A final episode in this story concerns the hospital bill. Upon Jesse's dismissal from the hospital, the hospital staff told the Gyamfis that the total costs would be approximately 32,000 U.S. dollars and that they would receive the bill in a few days. The bill for just the time Jesse was in ICU came to about 14,530 dollars. However, when the bill arrived a few days later, it was for the grand total of 0 yen. They owed absolutely nothing! God had worked another miracle!

After three years in the U.S. Marine Corps and one year in college, Richard Lucas attended Apostolic Bible Institute, where he met his wife, Jean. They assisted, evangelized, and pastored in the Leeward Islands as associates in missions and were furlough replacements in Guam before arriving in Japan in 1984.

During their first term, the Lucases established three military churches and led several Japanese people to the Lord. Eventually their appointment expanded to include ministry to Japanese nationals.

The Lucases pastor a church in Tokyo with three congregations (Japanese, internationals, and American military personnel). They have also opened two other national works now pastored by ministers working with them. They have been active in writing tracts and a training program, which is producing good results. Since his appointment as the superintendent of the UPC in Japan, Brother Lucas travels extensively throughout the country in evangelism, training, and organizing for continued growth of the rapidly expanding work.

Chapter 8

Korea: Kaleidoscope of Korea

By **Elton Bernard**
Former Missionary to Korea

Seoul, Korea

It was three weeks to remember. Beginning Easter Sunday, a former trinitarian pastor brought twenty-two of his members, whom he had only recently baptized in the trinity, to our headquarters to be rebaptized in the name of the Lord Jesus Christ. Two weeks later I baptized twenty-six more people, and thirty received the Holy Ghost.

The next day, amid rain and windstorm, we began a five-night, fourteen-service revival at a camp near Seoul. The devil offered many obstacles and much resistance, but our Holy Ghost-anointed evangelist preached the unadulterated Word without fear or trembling. The results were that more than 100 people were filled with the Holy Ghost as evidenced by speaking in other tongues, and 145 people were baptized in Jesus' name. The following weekend, in our headquarters church, nine people in the Sunday school and two more in the adult service were born of the Spirit as they began to speak in other tongues.

Our Seoul crusade began the next day. Much prayer and fasting on both sides of the Pacific had gone up for this meeting. Yes, there were miracles of healing and of salvation. During the five nights, 150 people received the Holy Ghost, and 174 were baptized in the name of the Lord Jesus! God healed several people before our eyes—we watched them stretch forth paralyzed arms and stand on unused legs.

The third week began, and it was amazing. Upon our invitation, 330 preachers from different denominations gathered for a week of an "introduction to Pentecost." They received a mighty demonstration of the power of the Holy Ghost. About thirty people received the Holy Ghost for the first time, and twenty-three were baptized in the name of Jesus!

Chunju, Korea

My wife and fellow missionary, Loretta, went to Chunju, a city about 120 miles south of Seoul, for a five-night revival. There were three services a day: 4:30 AM, 10:30 AM, and 7:30 PM. Being February, the weather was very cold, and she had to wear layers of clothing.

Korean bedrooms are heated by a low grade of compressed coal placed in a burner under the floor. The hot exhaust is funneled through a tunnel network, thereby heating the floor. Upon showing Sister Bernard her room, the pastor expressed his regrets that the heating system was apparently not working and that the room was not warm. There was nothing for her to do but to sleep in all of her woolens and her overcoat. That night she went to bed about midnight.

Someone had died next door, and the relatives were offering wine to the departed spirit of the man and were apparently offering a bit to themselves, too. Sister Bernard awakened at about 2:00 AM because of the noise. As she smelled something strong, her mind said, "Investigate," but her body would not move. At 4:15 AM she heard the alarm calling everyone to the dawn service. She thought, Grab your Bible, slip on your dress, pat your hair, and be gone. Her body, however, would not cooperate.

In a few minutes someone found her and pulled her out of the room. It was snowing. The humidity was high and the deadly coal fumes had lingered in the room. Her body was swollen and she was unconscious. The saints massaged her all day and kept her face covered with wet cloths. A substitute had to fill in for the two morning services.

Toward evening her senses began to return, and the church began to fill to capacity because posters were everywhere announcing that a Pentecostal missionary was going to preach that night. How can a Pentecostal be sacked out, half conscious, whenever she is suppose to be preaching? Sister Bernard said, "I'll preach tonight." The saints did not know how she would be able to preach, but they dragged her to church nonetheless. Clinging to the walls, she staggered to the pulpit—her body swaying, her head whirling. While she held on to the pulpit, it seemed as if she would faint.

But the Spirit of the Lord moved! She preached for an hour. It was the best service of all. People received the Holy Ghost, healings took place, and many people were "slain" in the Spirit for more than three hours. God heals! God saves!

Saturday morning after the last "amen," Sister Bernard was determined to take the first bus home. But, alas, her schedule was wrong and she had to wait for the next bus. After about an hour of travel, the second bus overtook the first bus, which had wrecked with many passengers badly injured. God protects!

The Testimony of Faithful Pentecostal Youth

Many high school students in our church started attending when they were in our elementary Sunday school. Most of them received the Holy Ghost and were baptized in Jesus' name during vacation Bible school revivals. But, oh, the persecution and the ridicule they endured from their parents! Most of the parents of our young people were non-Christians. They were usually Buddhist, Shamanist, or Confucianist. Many of them violently opposed their children's coming to church. However, our kids were faithful and God rewarded them. Here are some testimonies.

A woman came to our service one night and wept all through it. After praying for some time, she testified, "I fought my children coming to this church. I tore up their Bibles and songbooks. I whipped them. My husband screamed, 'We've thrown our kids away to that church.' But finally, I decided I can't win them back, so I might as well join them."

Another young man began coming to our church when he was eight years old. His mother told the missionary, "I've opposed him going to church. I have fussed so much until he would leave the house just to quit hearing me nag. He spent his nights at church or with church friends many times to avoid my opposition. However, through it all, he was a model son, and all the neighbors would tell me how blessed I was to have such an obedient son." She just could not keep fighting his Christian example. Now she is in the church with the baptism of the Holy Ghost.

Another little boy used to throw rocks at our tent when we first started years ago. Later he came into our Sunday school, received the Holy Ghost, and was baptized in Jesus' name. Soon he led his older sister and two brothers to church. His mother would scream at them, "You used to throw rocks at that church, and now you are going there. Get out of this house!" However, she is now in the church and a faithful supporter.

The Demilitarized Zone

One of our Bible school students was drafted into the Korean army. He went through intense persecution for his faith in God. He was stationed on the front lines in Korea and forbidden to sing or to pray aloud. There was no place for him to go to church.

Finally, he was moved a short distance away from the demilitarized zone, which separates North and South Korea, and was allowed to attend a small denominational church in the area. I received an urgent call to visit him. When we met, he and I had a Holy Ghost prayer meeting in the car, parked on a lonely, snow-packed road. In tears he related how that his conscience hurt him so badly because he was not able to worship in spirit and in truth. With our guidance he was able to secure permission from his company commander to have his own service in the camp mess hall. At first just seven people attended. Gradually it grew to around forty men. Hardly any of the men knew how to behave in church or how to kneel or to pray or to sing songs. Some of the officers of the company attended.

God began to move and to bless. Many of the men stopped smoking and drinking. Others began to apologize to our Pentecostal soldier whenever they smoked. The work expanded, and the young man wrote to his parents for a little money to rent a small room in the nearby village to start our own Pentecostal preaching point. In the first service, sixty-five people were present, including the company commander. The company commander told me that our Pentecostal soldier had proven himself to be a real Christian, so that now he had assigned him to no other duty but to minister to the men in the camp.

Summing Up

Here are the words of a second grader: "When my Sunday school teacher laid hands on me, my hands began to shake and I spoke in tongues and received the Holy Ghost. When I went outside, all of the flowers and the trees looked at me happily. It looked like heaven to me. My steps, oh, my steps were light, too. I went home, and while I was doing my work, a song kept coming out. When I met my friends, I wanted to tell them about receiving the Holy Ghost. I wanted to tell mom and dad, too!"

Elton and Loretta Bernard were appointed as pioneer UPCI missionaries to Korea in 1963 and arrived in August 1965. Their mastery of the Korean language was a valuable asset to the success of the work, and their translation of literature helped the work to progress even more rapidly. Besides being engaged in Bible school work, the Bernards were also responsible for supervising all of the churches. After resigning from foreign missions service in 1985, they founded an English church and a Spanish church in Gonzales, Louisiana.

Chapter 9

Nepal: A Hindu Finds Christ

By Deepak Kumar Shahel
Submitted by **Stanley K. Scism**
Missionary to South Asia/United Kingdom

Born and brought up in a Hindu family, I was dearly loved by my parents and relatives. As the firstborn son, I always eagerly fulfilled the demands of this position. Increasingly, however, my father devoted his life to drinking, gambling, and fighting. Beating his family became a daily routine. He gave up his job in the army, sold his business dealings, and therefore we became very poor. Still, he thirsted for religious truth, so he wandered from religion to religion, searching for salvation, but without peace or joy.

One day, he bought some sweets from a street-side stand. The paper on which the sweet was served was a tract. While he read this, the Holy Spirit moved on him, and he accepted Jesus Christ. All this occurred in 1967-68.

Two years later, my mother also accepted Jesus Christ. My father then went to Bangalore to study God's Word. Meanwhile, my Hindu grandmother took me into her house, and I mingled with many Hindu friends. Since my father wasn't there to control me, I joined a gang of Hindu street boys. Now stealing, fighting, drinking, and gambling became my daily routine. I abandoned school and focused on hating Christians, their faith in Jesus, the name of Jesus, my father, my family, and the church.

I later joined the Communist Party. Eager to torture my family and other Christians, I gave my life over to be trained in black magic to harm others through uttering evil words and spells, which we had to learn as fluently as possible and utter in one breath. Being obsessed with obtaining evil power and having the devil as an intimate partner, I began offering my own blood as a sacrifice by cutting my hand. With this evil art, I considered myself someone great, and I used these abilities to meet my necessities of life and to lure girls. After dating many girls, I truly fell in love with one and wanted to marry her at all costs. I knew she was Hindu, but I didn't consider my parents' wishes. My sweetheart, however, betrayed me and went to someone else; I had never expected this.

I plotted to take revenge but failed for the first time in my life. My friends called me a coward, and I began to hate myself. I attempted suicide by eating three hundred grams of poison. As I struggled between life and death, vomiting every two minutes for twelve hours, the question flashed in my mind each time I rose to vomit: Will I live or die? Surely I would die. Nobody ever lived after swallowing even thirty grams of this poison. But God, in His mercy and grace, kept me alive. He loved me because He had made me in His own image. He created me with His own holy hands. He did not want me to perish, though I wanted to.

Exhausted and totally unconscious because of all the vomiting, I did not know who was around me. But I knew that my spirit stood before God. I saw Him as a bright, sunlike figure. I felt God's hand holding me, and I was following Him. He led me into mysterious places, the unseen world of life after death. I trembled with fear—I didn't want to face God's wrath and torment in hell. I cursed every moment of my life on earth since it was too late for me to repent now. I could only accept God's final judgement. I saw Satan, the prince of darkness, smile at me, wanting me to be soon in his company. I heard him say, "Come, come, you wretched beast." I saw a company of demons dancing around me and the devil himself trying to pounce on me.

But God took me away from these frightful sights, stood me before Him, and said to me, "Now you will live again; I give you life to do My will. I have chosen you to bear fruit. You are My servant. Go in peace." I woke to see the bright, clear sun, to feel its warmth, and to hear the birds sing. It was 6:40 AM, March 26, 1980.

Alive with a new purpose, I sat on my bed and prayed to God. I had missed His company these last eight years. I studied Holy Scripture, discipleship, and spiritual warfare. This last subject Satan tried to use to hound me. One night in a dream I was forced to worship evil spirits as I had worshiped them in my past life. But I met this temptation with God's Word and prayer.

The Holy Spirit came to me one night and warned me to check myself again and to be aware of things in my possession. I still had part of a deer horn and skull, which I had used to utter evil words while casting spells, and an evil-looking mask, which I had used to substitute for the devil himself as a friend. I cried to Jesus for mercy and confessed to having these things still in my possession. I gave them up to be burned.

On January 1, 1991, I committed my life to God's work. I gave up my school and my side business and left my property, family, wife, son, and friends to serve the Lord. I went to Nepal to serve God among my native people, who are still unaware of this salvation and still worship the devil.

Since I was Pentecostal, the churches and other missions in Nepal did not welcome me, but God, nevertheless, met my needs. I prayed that God would give me true Christian fellowship somewhere. With the Holy Spirit's full guidance, I met Jesus Name people and a UPCI pastor on December 2, 1994. I had fellowship with him, and we prayed together and shared our joys and sorrows. I felt in my heart that I had met a true disciple of Jesus and a true friend. I received water baptism in Jesus' name on February 24, 1994.

Now I go on tract distribution and home visiting and personal contacts. I have converted two families and three young people. I want to serve the Lord full-time and pray that God will open a way for me so that I can be free from the school I teach in. The Nepal harvest is plentiful, but laborers are few. Pray for Nepal. I want my testimony to praise God, to show His love for me, and to declare that I owe my life to Jesus Christ.

Stanley Scism is the third generation of Scisms to do missionary service in India. He was appointed 1987. He is currently appointed to South Asia and the United Kingdom. For the back cover of his latest book he wrote:

"Stanley Scism founded, presides over, and teaches in the Scism Christian Institute, named, sadly, not for him but for his grandfather, Ellis Scism. At this writing, he serves as the area coordinator for India and Nepal, field superintendent, project coordinator, institution president, teacher, biography and commentary and newsletter writer, song lyricist, inviter of speakers, host of visitors, helper of little old ladies across the street, and partridge in a pear tree. He likes teaching, writing, reading, eating chocolate, praying, visiting prehistoric sites, making music programs, and witnessing."

Chapter 10

Dominican Republic: Brother Agustin's Shack

By **Jerry Burns**
Missionary Evangelists

With sustained winds of 140 miles an hour, Hurricane David ripped through the Caribbean in 1979, leaving a horrendous path of destruction. The original forecast was for the hurricane to pass to the south of Haiti and the Dominican Republic on the island of Hispaniola. At the last moment, however, it made a ninety-degree turn to the north and roared right through the center of Santo Domingo, the capital of the Dominican Republic. Thousands of Dominicans were surprised and trapped in their homes by the fiercely blowing winds.

Brother Agustin was a simple and uneducated man but one with tremendous faith in God. As the winds began to blow debris up against his little humble shack, he thought that his time to die had come. In his simple, childlike faith, he made a decision: "If I'm going to die, the very least I can do is to die praying!" Lifting up his hands to heaven, he began to worship and to call on the name of Lord. After a while, he became lost in the Spirit, and the Spirit began to make intercession for Brother Agustin. For at least four hours, Hurricane David wreaked terrible destruction and havoc on the city of Santo Domingo, destroying many heavily reinforced structures, while Brother Agustin prayed in his plywood-and-tarpaper shack.

After the winds subsided, Brother Agustin came to himself. Looking around, he was surprised that he was still alive. Running outside to see what had happened to his neighbors, he discovered total and utter destruction in every direction as far as his eye could see. But right there in the middle of all that destruction, sticking out like a sore thumb, was Brother Agustin's little shack. Not a piece of wood or tarpaper was out of place! Hurricane David left over 5,000 Dominicans dead and over 250,000 without homes. However, the shack filled with praise and worship withstood the storm.

Jerry and Beth Burns had the unique distinction of being appointed to the mission field on their first wedding anniversary at the 1972 General Conference in Miami, Florida. They spent the next fifteen years as missionaries to Venezuela and to the Dominican Republic. While in the Dominican Republic, Brother Burns served as field superintendent, and the church grew from six churches to forty-two churches.

From 1986 through 1997, Brother Burns served at the World Evangelism Center in Hazelwood, Missouri, involved in the areas of purchasing, cost control, and stewardship. The Burnses were reappointed as UPCI missionaries at the 1996 San Antonio General Conference, coincidentally on their twenty-fifth wedding anniversary. They currently serve as missionary evangelists at-large.

Brother Burns also serves as coordinator of Multimedia Ministries, a ministry that prepares audiovisual presentations to help missionaries communicate their burden and work more effectively to the home constituency.

Chapter 11

El Salvador: God Is Our Protector

By **Bruce A. Howell,** Regional Director
Central America/Caribbean

We heard the attack begin on the morning of November 23, 1989, at 4:00 AM. We were accustomed to hearing gunfire, bombs, helicopters, airplanes, and all that goes with a civil war. However, the intensity of this attack was different. The communist guerillas had been attacking the rest of the city for two weeks. We had brought the women from our church who were either very old or mothers with newborn infants to our home to get them out of the areas of the city that were being attacked. We thought that our part of the city was safe. We were wrong.

We all awoke to sounds of gunfire, helicopters flying overhead, planes shooting, and bombs exploding. In a few moments the electricity went out. The phones worked until about 7:00 AM, and then the lines were cut.

Our son, Jared, was staying at the Monte Showalters' house, a block and a half away. When the sun came up, I stuck my head out of the door and then walked to the end of the driveway. When I looked to the left, I saw an M16 pointed at me from the end of the block. I went back inside. When the gunfire would erupt, we could literally hear the bullets flying over the house, making a whining sound.

We started to pray, asking God for direction. I called everyone into the living room—seventeen people were in our house—and we began to pray. People were sitting in the room of our youngest daughter, Amy. Sister Luz de Ascension was sitting in the corner. Literally seconds after I called them into the living room, a bullet came through the ceiling and struck the wall in that corner. If she had still been there, she would have been killed. We have that bullet as a memorial to the protection of our God. I am glad there are no "ifs" with our God.

Bullets began to enter the house, and we moved everyone into the kitchen, the only room that had a second floor and a concrete ceiling. We sat around the walls and sang and prayed. We could hear the army cursing the guerrillas just a few feet from where we were. Our house did not have a wall in front of the house. The guerrillas had gotten into the houses all around us and had taken the people hostage.

I went to the second floor and looked out the window. I saw an F-14 fighter plane fly straight up, turn around, head straight down, and shoot missiles into our neighborhood. I went back down to the kitchen. When the shooting became more intense, I put my two daughters, Leah and Amy, under the kitchen cabinets that were made of concrete.

All of a sudden we heard a very loud explosion and the sound of glass breaking and realized that a bomb or missile had come into the house. The glass in the kitchen window shattered, and shrapnel went everywhere. At that time the ladies began to scream.

I will never forget what my daughters asked me at that moment: "Daddy, are we going to die?" I really do not remember all of my feelings at that moment. You can imagine how I felt, but I did not hesitate to tell them, "Everything is going to be all right. Jesus is with us."

We later learned that whatever had gone off had come through the wall of the house and exploded in the upper patio. This was an area where we hung out our clothes on the second story. There was an opening to the bottom where our water tanks and two butane tanks were. The hot shrapnel penetrated everything in the area except for the two butane bottles of gas.

Later on that day, the husbands of two of the young mothers were able to get into our house. They wanted us to take a white flag and leave. I told them that all could leave, but I would not leave without my son. The problem was that he was in an area controlled by the guerrillas, and we were at the edge of where the military was in control. The only thing we could do was take a white flag in a lull in the shooting and go get him. We left and the military and the guerrillas asked us what we were doing.

We got to the Showalters' house and I told them to get some things together to leave. During this time people were filtering out of our house little by little with white flags. My daughters had left with some saints while I was getting the Showalters and Jared. We put ketchup on one sister. When we wanted to leave, we told the soldiers that we were taking her out. They thought she was wounded.

When we got to the corner below my house, the military told me I could not go back to the house because they were going to open fire again. I told them that my wife was still in the house and I had to get her out. She had waited until all the others had left. They held their fire, and I was able to get her out.

When we got to the end of the road where there was no more fighting, we could not find our daughters. Curfew was at 6:00 PM, and we did not know where to go. I sent the Showalters to a hotel, and I went to find my girls. They were at the church, and I had about fifteen minutes to get to the hotel where the rest of my family was. The hotel, which was buzzing with people, had no rooms available. Finally, a clerk asked a journalist to let us have his room, and ten of us checked into the room.

I did not want to leave El Salvador, but a fellow missionary who understood the situation called Brother Harry Scism, the general director of Foreign Missions. I was told we had to leave. I went to Guatemala for two days, left my family, and came back. We were able to get out of the airport because of a friend who worked for the Salvadorian airline, TACA. We were afraid to drive because there was fighting in the entire country. After that, the devil attacked me, telling me that I had ruined the lives of my children by raising them in a war. But as always, the devil is a liar! I am glad to tell you that today over 76,000 constituents are in the church in El Salvador. I am so glad I learned that He is our protector!

Upon the recommendation of the Foreign Missions Board, the General Board of the United Pentecostal Church International appointed Missionary Bruce A. Howell to serve as the regional director for Central America/Caribbean Region. He filled the position vacated by Lloyd Shirley's appointment as the director of Education/AIM in May 1999.

A former dean of Christian Education at Jackson College of Ministries, Bruce Howell and his wife, Diane, received their missionary appointment to El Salvador in

May 1979. After studying Spanish in Costa Rica, they arrived in El Salvador in October 1980.

For twelve years they lived in a civil war that took the lives of 80,000 people and saw God's mighty hand protect them hundreds of times in battles, some in front of their home. Brother Howell had oversight of the entire national work, taught in the Bible school, and pastored the headquarters church. He also trained national leadership to assume the work and declined to allow his name to stand for election for the presidency of the UPC of El Salvador in 1999.

Sister Howell was the ladies leader of the country. She also directed the day school.

In 1993 Brother Howell was appointed as the superintendent of Honduras. He also directs the Honduran Bible school. He retains these responsibilities in his new position as regional director.

Chapter 12

El Salvador: The Van That Flew

By **Bruce A. Howell**, Regional Director
Central America/Caribbean

Earlier in the afternoon, Sister Howell and I had decided to visit the T. Wynn Drost family, the founding missionaries of the Salvadorian church who had recently moved to Guatemala. During this time of civil war in El Salvador, the guerrillas would block the roads by digging trenches, by putting logs across the road, or by putting large rocks in the way so no one could get by. When a vehicle would stop, the guerrillas would ambush it and do whatever they wanted to the occupants.

It was dark as we traveled that night in the mountains on a narrow, two-lane road. All of a sudden we came around the corner and saw large boulders in the road. I knew immediately that men were hiding in the weeds along the road.

We were going up the side of a mountain. A dropoff was on the left side. A wall of rock and dirt was on the right. There was no place to turn around. We were driving a Toyota Hiace, a four-cylinder van that did not sit high off the ground. There was no way we could make it over the large rocks that were across the road. The only human option was to stop and face the consequences of what would take place. I had my wife with me and knew what the guerrillas would do to her. In that moment, we only knew to call upon the name that is above every name, Jesus! There was no time to pray long prayers, no time to devise alternate plans, no opportunity to figure things out—just a couple of seconds to call upon that name. The Bible says that name is a "strong tower" (Proverbs 18:10). The demons know that name and tremble at the mention of it. That name delivers from sin and gives power to overcome temptations. As we called out on that name, I will never forget what happened!

I feel that God told me just to keep the "pedal to the metal" and not do anything else. I do not know if you believe in angels, but the Bible says that the angel of the Lord encamps around those who fear Him (Psalm 34:7). All of a sudden, I felt the car lift up and we began to fly over the rocks! I have never forgotten that feeling of flying over the rocks. I am sure those men were ready to come out and see what prize they had, but their eyes became very large as they saw, for the first time in their lives, a flying Toyota van. We flew over the rocks and went on our way.

You may be facing an obstacle in your life that seems insurmountable. I want you to know that the same God who provided angels to lift our van over the rocks is by your side right now. He will lift you over whatever the enemy has put in the roadway of your life. Just call upon Jesus' name. Victory is yours!

See biographical sketch of Bruce and Diane Howell on page 52.

Chapter 13

El Salvador: A Lesson in Humility

By **Scotty Slaydon**
Missionary to El Salvador

While I served as an associate in missions in El Salvador, my finances were almost always a point of much prayer, desperation, and hope. One Sunday evening after the worship service, I went to a fast-food restaurant to get some chicken. The driver-side window in my truck had been broken. I did not have the money to fix it, so I covered it with a piece of plastic in case of rain.

When I got to the restaurant, an elderly man was there begging and offered to watch the truck. I told him that if he would watch the truck, then I would bring him a meal from the restaurant. After eating and going out to give the "watchman" his meal, I found that he had gone. Oh well, he must have not wanted to wait. Getting into the truck I noticed that my jacket was missing. As it was pouring down rain, I postponed looking for it until later. After arriving home and looking for the jacket, there was still no sign of it. I could only conclude that the "watchman" had taken the coat as his pay instead of a meal.

Now that really made me mad. It was my best coat and went with three pairs of pants that I had. That was something very important for me. Later that night, the thought just would not leave me, and I could not believe that he would do such a thing when I had offered to help him. So I got up and went back to that area of the city.

Around 10:00 PM I was strolling the back streets looking for my coat and the man who was wearing it. About half an hour later there he was, with the coat! I almost could not believe my eyes. Sure, I went looking, but that was more to satisfy myself that I had done everything possible. When I confronted the man, he said that he was holding it for me until I returned. I proceeded to tell him that because of his attitude he probably would not get much help from other people and that he should be honest. I let him know that theft was wrong and a sin. About that time, some men unloading doughnuts nearby ran the guy off because he was loitering. I was satisfied because my coat was back in my possession.

While I was driving home, the Lord began to talk to me, and my conscience chastised my action. "But, Lord," I responded, "that was my best coat. You know that I don't have money to go around throwing coats to every beggar on the street. And besides, that man did wrong in taking my coat." It sounded like a good answer to me until the Lord spoke, "How much have I forgiven you? What shape were you in when I found you? When I was on the cross, it wasn't for any wrong that I had done. But I forgave them." Yikes!

Making a quick U-turn, once again I went looking for the "watchman." Of course, the Lord let me find him so that I could apologize. When the man saw me, he began to apologize. I stopped him and asked his forgiveness for my attitude. He was somewhat stunned, but he accepted a sandwich and hot coffee from a local diner.

And I learned a lesson in humility.

Scotty Slaydon first went to El Salvador in June 1987 as a student at Jackson College of Ministries. He returned in May 1989 to begin three and one-half years of service as an associate in missions. During his AIM tenure, Brother Slaydon became involved in youth ministry, local and national evangelism, Bible school, tent ministry, and many other areas of the work.

Receiving his full missionary appointment to El Salvador in October 1992, Brother Slaydon was named as director of the Bible school and continues to function in this capacity. He and Krista Forgues married in July 1994. Sister Slaydon has taught in the elementary school and is today in charge of the national bookstore. The Slaydons travel to different churches across the country each week to minister. Their involvement includes local, sectional, district, and national ministry.

Chapter 14

Guyana: God Sent It—Let's Grab It!

By **Janeace Miller**
Missionary to Guyana

While serving as associates in missions in Guadalajara, Mexico, we found ourselves almost broke. We had the equivalent of ten U.S. dollars. Our rent was due. We needed groceries and gasoline. Knowing that ten dollars would certainly not cover it all, we stood on the promise of God that He would supply all of our needs. After praying in the morning, my husband, Jerry, felt he knew how God would supply the need. He told me, "God has probably spoken to someone in the States, and they have sent us an offering in the mail. I am going to the post office and collect our miracle." He got there so early he had to wait for the post office to open. When he checked our box, it was empty! He could hardly believe there was nothing there. He came back to our apartment and told me, "Nada," meaning nothing.

Since a missionary family was moving into the city and another moving out, we got into our little Ford Festiva and went to help with all the moving. It was about 8:00 AM, and with six million people in that city, the streets are always packed solid with traffic and people. As we turned onto the four-lane boulevard, it looked very strange as only one car was ahead of us and a large truck was parked on the side.

As we drove down the empty street we noticed what looked like a big pile of leaves that someone had dumped in the middle of the road. When we got closer, a gentle wind blew the pile, and we saw that it was purple, not green like leaves. Purple is the color of a fifty-thousand-peso note! To our amazement, it was a huge pile of nothing but fifty-thousand-peso notes. Jerry slammed on the brakes without even bothering with the clutch, bringing us to a jerky stop.

He hollered, "It's money! Let's get it!"

It scared me so badly that I said, "No! It's probably drug money, and someone will shoot us."

"Drug money, my foot," he said. "God sent it. We need it. Let's grab it!" So we hopped out and began to gather all the money. During all of this time, no traffic came. We picked up 1.2 million pesos, which was the equivalent at that time of around five hundred dollars.

We got back in our car and drove to Missionary Michael Edge's home, and Jerry showed Brother Edge his wallet that was so stuffed that he could not bend it. Brother Edge said, "Man! Where did you get all that money?"

Jerry said, "Ah, it was just blowing down the street."

The first thing we did was pay our tithes. Then Jerry got worried that possibly some poor person had saved the money and maybe a child had thrown it out of the car window. We could not figure out how it got there. So he went back to where we had found the money and watched to see if he could see anyone looking distressed. He even went to the stores nearby, but he did not see or hear anyone talking about losing the money.

Maybe an angel from heaven came, stopped the

traffic, and dumped a basket of manna from heaven right in our path. However it got there, God sent it. We needed it. We grabbed it.

God may not supply in the way that you expect, but He always supplies.

Both Jerry and Janeace Miller received the Holy Ghost in Houston, Texas, at Bethel Tabernacle under the ministries of Brothers O. F. Fauss and O. R. Fauss. For twenty-three years the Millers pastored in the Texas, Texico, and Louisiana Districts and served as associates in mission in Mexico and the Caribbean.

The Millers' missionary involvement began in 1985 with an evangelistic trip to Brazil. In 1989 they became associates in missions to Mexico, basing out of the city of Guadalajara. Their later Associates In Missions assignments took them to the Caribbean where they ministered in Puerto Rico, the Dominican Republic, Trinidad, St. Kitts and Nevis, Bahamas, Barbados, and Guyana.

The Millers received their missionary appointment to Guyana in January 1998. They arrived in Guyana in January 1999.

Chapter 15

Guyana: The Miraculous Blackout

By **Loren D. Miller**
Associate in missions to Guyana

"Behold, I send an angel before thee, to keep thee in the way, and to bring thee into the place which I have prepared" (Exodus 23:20).

We arrived at church on a Wednesday night and set up the PA equipment as usual. I started the service off with prayer, and we began to pray that the Lord would do something in the service. As I began to lead the service in worship, a man walked in wearing only a white jagged cloth around his waist and carrying a bottle of whiskey that was almost empty. He was about six feet three inches tall and weighed 230 pounds of solid muscle. He began to grit his teeth, snarl, point a finger at me, and growl. As he started up the aisle towards me carrying his bottle, I looked out at the audience and realized that I only had twenty-five women and two small, short men present that night. The only thing I could do was call on Jesus!

I stopped everything and started binding that spirit. Immediately the electricity went out. When this happened, the man hastily left the building. I thought that we had merely gone into a blackout, which is quite common in Guyana. But when I looked out of the doors of the church, I realized that ours was the only building in blackout. About five minutes later when the man was gone, the electricity came back on, and we had an awesome service. Let me tell you that Jesus takes care of His kids!

Loren Miller, the son of Jerry and Janeace Miller, and his wife Felicia, went as associates in missions to Guyana to assist his missionary parents in February 1999. He pastors the church in Mon Repos, edits *TEAM* magazine, conducts tent crusades, and is involved in the printing ministry. He stated, "We are seeing people repent, baptized, and filled with the Holy Ghost, and some report being healed. Just recently a man was healed of severe kidney stones."

Chapter 16

Jamaica: The Revival in Golden Grove

By **Rachel Smith**
Former Missionary to Central America/Caribbean

This story is written in faith that it will encourage others not to look upon what is visible to the eye but to see the unseen. "Who hath believed our report? and to whom is the arm of the Lord revealed? For he shall grow up before him as a tender plant, and as a root out of a dry ground" (Isaiah 53:1-2).

When I reflect on Jamaica, I think of the years I was there from 1959 to 1962 when my husband and I were missionary evangelists. Brother A. D. Varnado, the former pastor of our home church in West Monroe, Louisiana, was the pastor of the headquarters church in Kingston, Jamaica, and superintendent of the district. He and his wife invited us to come and help them. We felt their burden and quickly responded to the need.

Paying our own way, we arrived and evangelized for three months in 1958. We returned the following year in October 1959 with a full missionary appointment from the Foreign Missions Division. We were equipped with a Sheaves for Christ car, a tent, a travel trailer, and a desire to bring revival to Jamaica. God blessed us with a ripe harvest field. From the headquarters church in Kingston to Ocho Rios, St. Ann's Bay, Glengoffee,

Trelawney, Warsop, Leachfield, Ulster Springs, Wakefield, Great Pond, Spicy Hill, Bamboo, Stanmore, Schoolfield, and Nutfield, souls were born into the kingdom throughout that beautiful tropical island in the West Indies. We also taught classes in the Bible school during several months of the year under the capable leadership of Sister Bessie Varnado.

Then with persistence and acceptance of the will of God, we went to Golden Grove. Bishop Varnado felt he should send us there even though this harvest field seemed to be burnt over. The pastor, his wife, and two other members were the only ones filled with the Holy Ghost. The pastor was discouraged and wanted to quit. It seemed that there was no use to continue. Although they and the missionaries did not know it, God knew that Golden Grove was a golden harvest field, ripe for the harvest of souls.

The pastor and his wife were to learn: "Feed your faith and doubt will starve!" They looked at the place where they were to pitch the tent and said, "If we alone are going to do the visitation, singing, and preaching, who will pray with the seekers when the altar call is given?" Nevertheless, Missionary Glen Smith was persistent: "You will see; God will work. Who will let Him?"

January 25, 1962, was a busy day of pitching the thirty-foot-by-fifty-foot tent and repairing the travel trailer's floor after the trip over rough country roads from Nutfield. The concrete blocks, which were to be used under wooden planks for the benches, had weighed on the springs of the car and caused the nineteen-and-one-half-foot travel trailer's floor to need replacing. Pastor Gallimore, Brother Wendell Ranken, and others came to put the new floor in. God faithfully provided the need, whether physical or spiritual.

It was time to begin the evening service. In a matter of moments, the townspeople began to hear the beautiful voice of Sister Jean Urshan and the choir singing, "It's harvest time. The Savior's calling. The grain is falling. Oh, do not wait; it's growing late...."

Jukeboxes played loudly that first night. One neighboring pastor drove by with his loudspeaker denouncing us as heretics. The opposition was working hard, doing overtime. For several nights the enemy told us, "I told you so. It's hot under the tent. Your voices are already tired, and your throats are raw from past revivals. It's useless to stay here."

For several evenings the ill-advised pastor drove around the community to raise his voice on the loudspeaker with sarcastic, mocking words at our attempt to bring revival. Our answer to his accusations was to place a Harvestime record near the microphone to spread the good news in song: "There Shall Be Light in the Evening Time." We simply ignored the enemy.

Finally persistence, trust, prayer, and faith in the Almighty brought fruit of repentance! A woman of ill repute came to the altar. Christy received the Holy Ghost the same night she first knelt at the altar and became a fervent altar worker from then on. Each following night, those she prayed through to the Holy Ghost became anointed to pray with seekers. Our voices became rested, clear, and strong to sing, pray, and preach with the unction that only the Spirit of the Lord can give.

Crowds filled the tent. The jukeboxes that were the nightlife of the community were hauled back to Kingston. The talk of the community was: "What's going on at the tent?" Some came to mock; others came hungry for a change of heart.

With so much excitement, we needed time to teach the basics of Christian living, so we announced morning prayer meetings. People came and God began to move in a special way. Ten young men came to mock, pointing at us and making sarcastic remarks. Almost immediately they were thrown from around the guide rope to inside the tent. That frightened them so badly that they began to cry aloud and to repent. God used that incident to have mercy upon their foolishness and to fill them with the precious Holy Ghost.

After this incident, it became noised around that we were sprinkling some kind of mystic powder that caused people to pass out under some kind of spell. However, it also became clear that people's lives were being changed by the dynamic power of the Holy Ghost. Each convert became a living testimony to the cleansing power of Jesus.

Pastor Gallimore, the brother of Bishop David Gallimore, passed a woman's house on his way to prayer meeting one morning and heard her screaming and crying from within. He stopped and called to her, asking if she needed help. She appeared at the door, her face red and her eyes puffy from crying, with tears streaming down her face. She screamed, "Oh, my God! Yes. Something is wrong with me. I am full of sin. I am living with a man that I'm not married to. I am throwing his things out of my house. There are his clothes in that bag. I'm not washing his clothes or cooking his food until he marries me. I have plans to go to that tent and get that power today so I will feel clean inside."

And it happened. We saw her come in, fall on her knees, repent, and receive the Holy Ghost that same morning. That night the man she had been living with came to the tent very upset. While standing with the crowd near one of the posts, he said, "If I go under the tent, down to the altar to please her, someone will have to throw me in there." He had hardly gotten the words out of his mouth, when to the astonishment of those around him, they saw him fall and somersault head over heels to the front of the pulpit.

A few nights later he stood to testify to his conversion. His words were electrifying. He said, "Do you see me? I am not what I used to be. I was a nobody, but now I am a somebody. God got a hold of this old boy. Now I am changed. I am inviting everyone to our wedding, and there won't be any liquor there. You will see that I am changed." Tears ran down the people's faces as they listened and shouted praises to God.

Grownups sent children to check around the microphone, the altar, and the pulpit for the powder that we were supposed to sprinkle. But they testified, "There ain't nothing there that I could see."

Many of the other churches came with some of their saints. After performing a wedding in Nutfield, Brother Varnado stopped by Ocho Rios and brought several saints from there and the surrounding area. They included Bishop and Sister Norman Houslin from Ocho Rios, Bishop and Sister David Gallimore from St. Ann's Bay, and Brother and Sister A. S. Palmer and several saints from Bamboo. Many other visitors and ministers came from different parts of Jamaica to rejoice in the spiritual blessings of the Lord. They came to taste and see the fruits of revival.

During that revival seventy-nine souls were baptized in the precious name of Jesus. Seventy-five of those received the Holy Ghost, and so there came the urgent need for a building. By June, with the help of Sheaves for Christ, we laid the foundation and built the concrete walls. At the end of the year, we held a dedication service to celebrate the glory of God.

Brother Varnado and Brother Smith spoke of the need of reaching the other islands of the Caribbean.

When Brother Smith and I returned to the United States, Brother Oscar Vouga, the director of the Foreign Missions Division, approached us about our burden and interest in the Spanish-speaking islands of Puerto Rico and the Dominican Republic. We met with the Foreign Missions Board, received our appointment at the General Conference in 1963, and set sail on a freighter the following February. We arrived on February 25 to speak a language we had not learned and to bring the gospel to other islands that had not received the true message of salvation. Puerto Rico became our base to reach out to all the other island nations of the Caribbean.

> Little is much when God is in it.
> Labor not for wealth or fame.
> There's a crown of life awaiting
> When you go in Jesus' name.

Harold Glen and Rachel Smith received their appointment as missionary evangelists in 1959. They first ministered in Jamaica and then transferred to Puerto Rico in 1964. Establishing a work in Puerto Rico and using it as a base, the Smiths reached out to the other nations of the Caribbean as the Lord opened the doors. Their ministry influenced the founding of the United Pentecostal Church in Puerto Rico, the Leeward Islands, Haiti, the Dominican Republic, and Trinidad and Tobago. They were involved in virtually all phases of developing and bringing these fields into maturity through evangelism, church construction, pastoral seminars, Bible school construction and instruction.

In 1984 the General Board of the United Pentecostal Church International ratified the appointment of Brother Smith as the regional field supervisor for Central America/Caribbean Region. They faithfully served as the regional field supervisor until their retirement in 1991.

They are now living and ministering in Louisiana.

Chapter 17

Belgium: Lydia's Story

By **Brenda Ciulla**
Missionary to Belgium

Lydia was a very devout Catholic, reared in a Catholic home by a pious Catholic mother. Throughout her life, spiritual things fascinated her. She wanted to know about anything that had to do with the spirit world.

As Lydia grew older and throughout her married life, she searched more and more for the things of God. As her two girls were growing up, she taught them to be good, moral people and to be good Catholics. At one time in her searching, Lydia even attended yoga sessions, trying to fill the spiritual hunger that she had inside. There just is something missing, she thought. There must be more to life than what I have. It was not that she was unhappy. She had a good husband who cared for her and gave her all the material things that she needed. She had a loving family, and they were very close.

Then one day her life changed. Her son-in-law's mother gave her a small Christian magazine to read since the mother was not interested in it. Lydia read it that day. She read an article about the importance of being baptized in Jesus' name. She continued reading the magazine, and for some reason, she kept being drawn to the article on baptism. In fact, every time she read about Jesus' name, it was like the name would stand out in bold print. She finally understood that this was for her. The baptism the article was talking about must be truth.

Finally she went to her priest and told him that she wanted to be baptized in Jesus' name as she had read about. He let her know that she had already been baptized as a baby; it was not necessary for her to be baptized again.

Lydia kept this in her heart a while and wondered what she could do to be baptized. Not too long after that, Lydia came in contact with a lady from our church. In their conversation Lydia started explaining to our sister about receiving this information on baptism in Jesus' name and that she wanted to find someone who would baptize her. Of course, our sister was happy to tell her what our church taught and told Lydia, "Our pastor will baptize you."

Lydia was so excited about meeting Brother Ciulla. When he gave her a Bible study on Jesus Name baptism, why we baptize in that name, and the importance of it, she wanted to be baptized right away. At first Brother Ciulla said, "I need to give you more studies so you can really understand." But Lydia said she wanted to be baptized right away.

The following Sunday she came to our church for the first time. Since she had never been in a Pentecostal-style worship service before, the service was totally new to her. Nevertheless, her desire to be baptized was strong. She soaked in everything that was going on in the service. When Brother Ciulla baptized her, she came up out of the water so happy.

Lydia did not understand everything, and being a faithful member of the church was something she needed to work on. We did not see her all the time, but every time she came, God blessed her greatly. Brother Ciulla would tell her, "You can have this more often." Finally one Sunday, Brother Ciulla preached on receiving the Holy Ghost and that the Holy Ghost gives us power to live a Christian life and power over sin and the enemy. That Sunday Lydia almost ran to the altar! She fell on her knees, and in a few minutes she was speaking in tongues and praising God.

With her new experience, Lydia became brave enough to invite her husband to church. Thinking he would not understand it, she had never invited him before. He was not even a devout Catholic as she had been. When he came for the first time, he did not know what to think. Seeing people clapping and raising their hands in church was unheard of to him. By the end of the service, however, he had started clapping his hands to the singing. After the service, he told Brother Ciulla what he had felt at first but that he was now enjoying it. Jean-Paul, Lydia's husband, started attending services with his wife every Sunday. One day when we had a baptismal service, he raised his hand and said, "Pastor, I want to be baptized, too!" How excited Lydia was to see Jean-Paul being buried in the name of Jesus. Not long afterward he received the Holy Ghost.

Since that time, Lydia's mother and father began coming to church. They both have been baptized, and her mother has received the Holy Ghost. We are still praying for her father to receive this experience.

Jean-Paul and Lydia are working in our new church in the city of Nivelles. They are a great help to Pastor Norroy in that city. We are so proud of them and happy for the Pentecostal experience they have received.

Lydia still prays for her children to receive the same experience. They can have it too!

Brenda Ciulla met her husband, Philip, at Conquerors Bible College. Brother Ciulla, a native of Sicily who was reared in Belgium, arrived in America in 1973 to study for the ministry. Following their marriage and his graduation from CBC in 1976, Brother and Sister Ciulla pastored in Washington State and evangelized in the Pacific Northwest. They received their appointment as UPCI missionaries to Belgium in October 1985.

Brother Ciulla returned home just in time to bid farewell to his dying pastor. The church that Brother Marcel Robin founded in Brussels has experienced tremendous growth under Brother Ciulla's leadership. He has also started four other churches and preaching points.

In 1996 the Ciullas' appointment expanded to include Switzerland and Italy, although he later asked to have Itlay removed from his portfolio. Brother Ciulla is fluent in English, French, and Italian.

Chapter 18

Eastern Europe: Where Angels Dwell

By **Samuel Balca**
Area Coordinator for Eastern Europe

Her name was Julia. She was born on July 18, 1908, in Poprad, Slovakia, and fell asleep for the last time on February 6, 1998, in Toronto, Canada. She was an extraordinary person, somewhat akin to an angel. I know. She was my mother.

My mother was virtually unknown by the public—such a contrast to her preacher husband whom the Lord used in many parts of Europe to propagate the gospel and to influence thousands. So what made my mother special? She was a praying woman. As a child, often I would see her on her knees and face in prayer. She wasn't just saying prayers; there was a holy hush—a shekinah glory—in the room where she prayed.

Many times as a child I would run through the house shouting, "Mommy, where is my . . . ?" And as I was about to run into her room, there was almost a physical presence, a hallowed atmosphere that I dared not disturb.

Since my mother's departure to glory, I relived those precious memories over and over and asked the Lord if it were possible for some of what my mother had to be transferred to me. First, the Lord gave me a brief glimpse behind the scenes in my mother's prayer

Samuel Balca, Julia Balca, Anne Balca Nowacki

room. I saw myself as a little boy running to her room as I did so many times before. Instead of seeing just the usual scene of my mother on her face on the floor praying, I also saw angels. Where the walls of the room were supposed to be, I saw row upon row of angels sitting quietly, all of their attention focused intently upon the kneeling, praying form of my mother.

Then I understood. My mother was at home in the presence of angels, worshiping the Lord. To her it was an everyday experience. No wonder there was always such an angelic aura about her—always levelheaded, full of joy, kind, and gentle.

Of course, she wasn't perfect. I remember that soon after the war, when the country was still recovering, we had a milking goat. Every evening my mother would milk the goat for our daily supply of milk. One particular evening the goat was acting up and kept knocking over the milk pail. Even my mother's seemingly endless supply of patience was sorely tested. She suddenly snatched up the three-legged stool she was sitting on and smacked the goat on the rump. Even this outburst was done with such angelic authority that the goat immediately calmed down until the milking was done.

My mother's life was anything but easy. She left the security of her family and country of Slovakia, married a man she barely knew, moved to Yugoslavia—for her, a new country and a different culture—and became a preacher's wife. Life was hard, but she knew her source of strength!

In the midst of trials and struggles, tragedy struck. She watched as her baby's life ebbed away in her arms. Her heart must have been broken as she carefully laid the little body down for the last time. But then there was the session with her Lord, where angels dwell, and she carried on without complaint. No depression, no hysteria, no questions, Why? She had a deep, settled, peaceful attitude like Job: "The Lord gave, and the Lord hath taken away; blessed be the name of the Lord" (Job 1:21).

Imagine her feelings when the police came yet again and took her preacher husband away for yet another interrogation or beating, with the unanswered questions left hanging in the air: "How will he return? Bruised and wounded? An invalid? A dead body? Will he return at all?" She felt fear—stark, cold, cruel fear—but she didn't panic. She didn't lose her mind. She just ascended to the level where angels dwell. There her Lord took her in His loving arms and comforted her, whispering encouragement and strength into her spirit, dispelling the anguish and pain, and replacing them with a calm assurance that Jesus was in control and that everything would be all right.

Eventually she had six children to care for, often alone because her husband was away preaching. And on top of that, she had to care for the family shoemaking business. She felt overwhelmed by the sheer volume of work and responsibilities, but she never despaired and never gave up.

Later on in life, her eyesight began to fade away until she was blind. She lost her sight, but she did not lose her salvation. She continued to be full of joy and happy songs because that is how people are when they spend much time in the presence of angels, worshiping the Lord. She was one of those fortunate souls who find out that one does not need natural eyesight to see the glories and beauties of the spiritual world.

How could my mother, a frail, weak, helpless woman, win such victories? She was at home in the presence of angels—that is, in the secret place of the Most High. I am trying to learn the same lesson, to be so full of God's glory and power that nothing in this world will be able to stop me or to discourage me. If I catch myself complaining about my lot in life, I just think of someone like my mother, and I quickly realize that I have no reason to complain. I just need to visit the place where angels dwell—in the presence of God.

Samuel Balca, a native-born Yugoslavian with Canadian citizenship, has a long-standing burden for the people of Eastern Europe. He and his wife, Patricia, who are both skilled linguists, have been involved in evangelizing and training Eastern Europeans since 1971. They received their appointment as United Pentecostal Church International missionaries to Eastern Europe in 1979. He serves as the area coordinator for sixteen nations of Eastern Europe.

Having completed their furlough in September 1998, the Balcas presently reside in Budapest, Hungary. They travel extensively throughout Eastern Europe. The collapse of communism in Eastern Europe has opened unlimited opportunities to encourage, evangelize, and train the 133 million people in lands formerly behind the Iron Curtain.

Chapter 19

The Netherlands: He Sent His Word and Healed

By **Michael Tuttle**
Missionary to the Netherlands

In October 1999 at the start of the General Conference of the United Pentecostal Church International in Nashville, Tennessee, I was admitted to a Nashville hospital due to a perforated colon and an abscess on the colon. The diagnosis was diverticulitis. I remained in the hospital for six days and received intravenous antibiotics. The doctor scheduled surgery for December 6.

The surgeon said the diseased colon would need time to rest in order to allow the infection and inflammation to come under control before he operated. The diseased portion of the colon would have to be removed surgically since there was no other way medically for it to heal.

Thank God for those who went to prayer on our behalf. Thank God for those He sent to the hospital to lay hands on me and to pray. Our regional director and his wife, Brother and Sister Robert Rodenbush, and our pastor and his wife, Brother and Sister Barry King, took time from their busy schedules to visit and to pray with me. Many others took time to call, visit, pray, or send a note of encouragement. Thank God for the body of Christ and the Word that heals. Thank God for the prayer of faith, the word of faith, and words of encouragement He sent through people of faith!

Sometime in the middle of November 1999, I received an assurance that healing had taken place and that I would not need surgery. Behind the platform and before the missionaries marched out for the General Conference missions service, they had prayed on my behalf. Later a missionary told Sister Tuttle, "Your husband will not need surgery." A pastor called long distance to say, "God has healed you, and surgery will not be needed." On the Thursday prior to the surgery, Brother Thomas, a worship leader in one of our churches in Holland told the church family that God had given him a dream that I would not be operated on. He then fell to the floor in prayer and in tears of thanksgiving. On that same Thursday in the surgeon's office in Nashville, I told the doctor that I believed that God had healed me and, therefore, I would not need surgery. The doctor told me that prayer was the only way this could be healed without surgery.

On Friday, December 3, 1999, the doctors did the necessary preoperation examination. The exam showed that the Healer had already been there. God had sent His word, and by the operation of faith, the disease was healed, the damage repaired, and the sick cured!

That evening the surgeon called to confirm that God indeed had done the work. Surgery would not be needed! It is a miracle of God's marvelous healing power!

Thank you to the many friends for praying! I am thankful that the Healer who heals all diseases sent His word and healed me. His name is Jesus. His healing power is alive in the world today!

Mike Tuttle's involvement in International Youth Corps in 1971 and 1972 helped to prepare him for missions work. After graduating from Conquerors Bible College in 1975, he worked for one year in Germany under the Foreign Missions Division's Missionary Helper program and the college's ministerial internship program. In 1982 he returned to Europe with his wife and young son to pastor a military church in Baumholder, Germany, under the Associates in Missions program.

In 1984 the Tuttles were appointed to the Netherlands. Since being in Holland, they have reopened the work in Hoofddorp, opened a new work in Zaandam, reestablished the work in Dordrecht, and begun an intensive training program.

Brother and Sister Tuttle reside in the small town of Zwijndrecht, south of Rotterdam near the church in Dordrecht. They went on furlough in September 1999.

Chapter 20

United Kingdom: Doing the Kangaroo Hop

by **Mervyn D. Miller**
Director, Faith Promise Ministries

It began as a regular, midweek Bible study service one Wednesday night while we were pastoring in London, England. We had not planned for a divine interruption. The good opening song service, as only precious Jamaicans know how to sing, was followed by prayer requests, the offering, and weekly announcements. We were cruising at the norm for a midweek service.

After an anointed solo by a fine young man, it was time for the Word. No one enjoys this better than I do, and to minister and to teach a church full of West Indian believers is in itself an exhilarating and thrilling experience.

Apparently unnoticed by all the worshipers, a lovely little English woman had slipped in the side entrance of the church and found a seat in the midsection of the sanctuary.

I was well into my Bible lesson, when to my surprise the English visitor began acting in an odd manner. Now, that's not necessarily strange in a Pentecostal service. It seems that we sometimes attract peculiar people, but there was something different in this instance.

The lady would stand up, wave her arms in the air, and promptly sit down again. For the first two or three times I simply ignored her and continued teaching. Then the woman, as if to say, "You are not noticing me," began doing knee bends, up and down, up and down.

My first feeling was to have someone move beside her and try to control those physical calisthenics, but, alas, I was too late. Since I failed to recognize her standing and waving and knee bending up and down, to my shock and dismay, she came down the aisle, not walking or running, but hopping! She was doing a kangaroo hop!

There, standing before my pulpit, was a soul whose need I had failed to see. She was still going through her actions of knee bending down to the floor and then back up again with her hands reaching into the air. "Can I say something?" she asked. Reluctantly I handed her the pulpit microphone, and with tears racing down her cheeks, she gave us this testimony:

"As I passed this church tonight on my way home from work, I suddenly realized that I could not cross the street to my apartment. Something literally caused me to come into this church. It was so strong that I could not resist. I know now that it was God who brought me here.

"You see, for seven years my right leg has been locked at the knee. When I walked I actually dragged the leg because there was no movement whatsoever. I sat in this service, not fully understanding everything, yet knowing God was in this place. Suddenly my knee was unlocked. It was as if two hands gently massaged the sides of my knee area, and the leg I had not bent in years was now loosed. You see, Pastor, that's why I have been standing up and bending to the floor. The Lord has performed a great miracle in my life!"

And off she went down the aisle doing her kangaroo hop, shouting, "Jesus did it! Hallelujah!"

Mervyn D. Miller was born in Belfast, Ireland, to devout Presbyterian parents. Young Mervyn's family was introduced to the power of Pentecost during a tent revival meeting, in which he was also healed of a childhood paralysis. In 1956 Brother Miller immigrated to America and traveled as an evangelist. Later, He married Marilyn Ruth Dyson in Little Rock, Arkansas.

The Millers pastored three churches in Arkansas, but the majority of their ministry has been in foreign missions. They were appointed as the first UPCI missionaries to the British Isles in 1964. They pioneered a work in London, and Brother Miller also served as superintendent of the Europe and British Isles Districts. After two terms in England, the Millers transferred to Italy to pioneer a work in Rome.

From Italy the Millers returned to Arkansas to pastor the Apostolic Church of Jesus Christ in North Little Rock. Five and a half years later they accepted the challenge of the Pacific Region and became a regional field supervisor in January 1984. From there he became the director of promotion for the Foreign Missions Division. He left that position to pastor in Nashville, Tennessee.

The Millers currently live in St. Louis, and he serves as the director of Faith Promise Ministries. With a full-time person directing the ministry and scheduling and holding services throughout the fellowship, Faith Promise is blessing more and more churches.

Chapter 21

Guam: Twenty-one Nations Hear the Gospel

By **Monte Showalter**
Missionary Evangelists

When we arrived on Guam to be with Missionaries John and Debi Wolfram in June 1999, the South Pacific Games, a pre-Olympic gathering for athletes competing for spots on Olympic teams, were in progress. God was doing a marvelous thing to reach athletes from twenty-one nations.

A new brother who was attending Brother Wolfram's church, Robert Celestial, worked as an aide to one of Guam's senators. Senator Calvos asked Robert to sit in on the planning meetings for the upcoming games in his stead. After days of meetings, Robert noticed that nothing was being considered for Christian athletes who were coming. He proposed that they set up a worship center. This had never been done before in existing games.

To his amazement, after a short discussion among the planners, they gave him a building in the athlete village to use. This was only one of many miracles along the way. Wisdom had to be used in order not to offend anyone in the Christian community. All supplies would have to be donated, and volunteers would have to be recruited to man the center. Amazingly, all the pieces came together like clockwork.

Volunteers, mostly from Pastor Wolfram's church, witnessed and passed out thousands of tracts, flyers, Bibles, and other pieces of literature during the two-week event. Several athletes were also a powerful force for truth as they shared their testimonies with their peers. Worship leaders conducted services each evening for the duration of the games. The worship center quickly became the hangout, not only for the Christian athletes but also for the unsaved.

On Thursday, June 10, 1999, Pastor Wolfram's church held an open-air meeting outside the worship center. God had given Brother Wolfram a plan to get more athletes to attend. He advertised the event to be the end-of-the-games "celebration." He announced by faith that there would be a mass choir composed of all the attending countries. Hundreds of handbills were passed out. This was to be a night of sharing and celebrating together!

The anointing was heavy on Sister Wolfram and the Pacific Revival Center Praise Team. As they continued to sing, more and more athletes began to gather around the tents. As the praise team sang a song about healing, the Spirit of God moved so mightily that Pastor Wolfram called on everyone in the audience to pray for each other as the singing went forth. Many people cried out to God and some lay prostrate on the ground. Several huge men broke down in tears. Several people testified later that they were healed.

When called to speak, I preached about the gospel of Jesus Christ. I explained that we appropriate the gospel by repenting, being baptized in Jesus' name, and receiving the Holy Ghost with the evidence of speaking in tongues. I led the whole group, now a good-sized crowd, in repentance.

We were feeling after the Holy Spirit for the right

time to pray with people to receive the Holy Ghost. Since we had promised several groups of athletes from different countries that they could sing, we were bound to our word.

A large group that was supposed to sing was from Fiji. Robert heard that a special meeting in their housing area was keeping them from coming to the worship center. He went to check it out. When he arrived, he saw someone who really seemed important speaking to the group. He obviously had the respect of a chief in their culture by the way the people were sitting around him on the ground. Someone told Robert that this man was a bishop of some kind of church.

Robert wanted to talk with this man but said it was like getting an audience with a king. He finally just boldly barged in and sat down next to him. The bishop asked him what he wanted, and Robert said, "I would like you to come to the worship center." The bishop got right up from the meeting and said, "Let's go." As they got up to go, everyone stood in respect to this man. As they walked across the grounds, people everywhere continued to stand in honor of him.

We found out later that this bishop had just flown for over twenty-two hours from the United States to Korea and then to Guam to watch his son compete in an event. As they walked into the worship center, Brother Wolfram invited him to testify right after the Fiji group sang. He turned out to be a godsend. This unforeseen guest testified with an incredible anointing! Since he was an islander, everyone listened with great respect. He preached to the lukewarm and to backsliders. He told the athletes that they needed to be on fire for God. He did not pull any punches!

Conviction fell on everyone. People who were listening nearby began to come out of the dorms. After testifying for about ten minutes, he wanted to turn it back to Brother Wolfram, but Brother Wolfram told him to keep preaching. The crowd confirmed it by yelling, "Preach! Preach!"

He went on to preach about Jesus, God coming in flesh, and about receiving the Holy Spirit with speaking in tongues. This was the break we were waiting for! Brother Wolfram asked him to bring the whole audience to the front to pray with each other. It was an awesome sight to behold. Backslidden athletes, sinners, coaches, nurses, and YWAM kids from Canada, Samoa, New Zealand, Australia, and the United States were all seeking God for the Holy Ghost together. Before the altar call was over, several people received the Holy Ghost for the first time, and many testified of being renewed in the Holy Ghost!

We never did get a chance to talk with the bishop. After he finished his message, he disappeared into the night just as quickly and mysteriously as he had appeared. Robert later told us that the bishop had requested a handful of the literature, originally prepared for the athletes, for himself.

The most wonderful thing about the whole two weeks was that we were able to personally put into the hands of almost 1,000 athletes from twenty-one different nations the Acts 2:38 message. Thanks to Pente-Com, we were able to pass out Simeon Young's wonderful tract *The Seven Steps to Salvation,* along with Bill Hobson's *Bible Study in a Bag* and Lewis Manuwal's tract *Jesus Name Baptism.* We sent the names and addresses that accumulated throughout the two weeks to our missionary friends throughout the Pacific.

Many of the athletes confided in Robert that they were really backslidden. They admitted to him how the worship center convicted them and brought them to a living relationship with Jesus Christ.

Below are just three of the many testimonies that were given to us.

From the gold medal winner in pole vaulting, Sera Vakaloloma of Fiji: "On the first day I arrived at the Games village, I noticed a sign board. It said, 'Worship Center.' I was really glad to know that we've got a place where we can go for our quiet time in the morning and singing and also an information center for the church services on Sunday.

"As I've been to two of the South Pacific Games, Mini South Pacific Games, and other games, this is the first time in history where we had a worship center organized at the games. Thank God for Brother Robert and his team.

"The worship center meant a lot to me."

From Emmeline L. Clochard, Vanuatu: "I play table tennis. God is so good! I've been blessed a lot through the worship center. Before coming to Guam, I prayed for months to know if it was God's will that I come. I felt it was His will, so I came. And it was a real blessing.

"I have been praying, asking God to baptize me with His Holy Spirit, and guess what! Last Sunday I received the baptism of the Holy Spirit at the Pacific Revival Center. At last God answered my prayer-and all through the worship center. Praise the Lord!"

Letter from Missionary Lee Sherry, Vanuatu: "It was great to hear from you—exciting, too. Your outreach at the South Pacific Games was wonderful. Thank you so much for sending us the names of those from Vanuatu. Winnie has already been contacted and there has been a good response. Her husband, who until last year was employed at the post office, wants to become a full-time minister. He is interested in Bible school and came this morning to sit in on some classes."

Monte and Dianne Showalter, former associate in missions instructors in the Haitian Bible school, received their appointment as UPCI missionaries to El Salvador in October 1986. Brother Showalter, who previously pastored in Wisconsin, was a full-time evangelist at the time of their appointment. His evangelistic ministry continued in El Salvador as he held tent crusades throughout the nation, helping begin forty-two churches.

In January 1992 the Foreign Missions Board appointed Brother Showalter as the field superintendent of Guatemala. As the field superintendent, he led the UPC of Guatemala to greater revival and growth. By May 1997 the Guatemalan church had grown from 5,000 constituents to 11,500.

In May 1997 the Showalters went on furlough and received their appointment as international missionary evangelists. They have conducted seminars in Central and South America, Guam, and Europe.

Chapter 22

Hawaii: Thankful

By **Sue Robertson**
Former Missionary to Hawaii

It was May 3, 1997. I was about to enter into one of the most difficult trials of my entire life.

We had just finished our Hawaii District Ladies Retreat with Fredi Trammell as the speaker. My husband, Rex Robertson, had suffered severe back pain for about two weeks, and then unbearable pain began in his stomach, with no relief. About 4:00 AM I took him to the emergency room, and he was admitted to the hospital.

For several days there was a conflict of opinion among the doctors about his illness. Then they found a mass lying in front of his pancreas. The doctors could not do surgery due to its location, for surgery would be fatal. A severe case of pancreatitis was the reason for the terrible pain.

One night my husband called for me to come back to the hospital. He was suffering so much that he said he could not bear it any longer. The doctors had already given him the strongest morphine they could give without shutting down his system—and it was not relieving the pain.

When my sister-in-law, Jan Saunders, and I got to

the hospital, we fell on our knees and began to pray. We called the World Network of Prayer, and people around the world began praying for us.

At about 6:00 AM the doctor came in and took me aside. He told me, "Mrs. Robertson, maybe I shouldn't tell you this, but if your husband has pancreatic cancer like we think he has, we can't do any more for him." I called our assistant pastor, Michael Johnson, and told him to call the church to prayer. Brother Robertson had not slept for four days and nights. When the church met that evening, they spent the whole service praying. That night my husband went to sleep and slept most of the night. When he awoke, the pain was gone, and he has never had it again. Praise God!

Two days later the doctors were able to get a biopsy. It had taken two and a half weeks. The doctors then told us that it was not pancreatic cancer, but non-Hodgkin's lymphoma, which was treatable with chemotherapy. After six chemotherapy treatments, the doctors did a CAT scan and found no sign of cancer. God worked a true miracle.

Ten months later we were back at the hospital. This time it was our daughter, Shelley. She was expecting her first child and was losing amniotic fluids. After being hospitalized a month, she had a little boy, Seth, at six months. He lived only fifteen hours. Shelley and her husband, Hugo, were devastated.

I'm glad my story does not stop there. As I write in this beautiful Christmas season 1999, I have much to be thankful for. Brother Robertson is feeling wonderful and has been cancer-free for two years! Shelley and Hugo are expecting another child close to Christmas. Though this pregnancy is high-risk, I know the same God, in whose hand I committed my husband, holds the life of this child. The greatest lesson learned through my hardest trials was to trust God and to no longer take each day for granted.

Rex and Sue Robertson were in their seventeenth year of pastoring the church he had founded in Neosho, Missouri, when they received their missionary appointment to Hawaii in 1986. In October 1995 Hawaii became an official district of the United Pentecostal Church, and Brother Robertson was elected its first superintendent in February 1996. In addition to his district duties, he and his wife still pastor the church they founded in Honolulu.

This story was reprinted from *Reflections*, November-December 1999. Used by permission.

Chapter 23

Papua New Guinea: Japheth's Miracle

By **Esther Henry**
Missionary to Papua New Guinea

On Sunday, March 10, 1996, after our morning worship service, a young couple asked us to pray for their baby. This couple lived in a very remote bush village and attended a church. Their baby, however, had been very ill for five weeks, so they came to us for prayer.

The baby's name was Japheth. He was only six months old, but he was at death's door. He had had severe diarrhea, vomiting, and urination problems for five weeks. His eyes were sunken, his belly was extremely swollen, and his ribs stuck out like a skeleton. In addition he was severely dehydrated. Sunday morning as I cradled that precious baby in my arms and prayed, I could feel that his skin was burning up with fever.

Japheth was in my thoughts continually. On Monday, March 11, I woke up with him on my mind. As I prayed for him, I asked God what I should do to help that little child. As I searched through the book *Where There Is No Doctor*, I became inspired as I read on preparing rehydration liquids and on the care of infants with high fevers.

Brother Walu, the man who had brought the couple to church, also drove a town bus. So after going to the market, buying some bananas, and preparing a liter of rehydration liquid, I sat on my verandah and waited for his bus to come to the bus stop across the street. When his bus came, I ran out of the gate and across the road and told Brother Walu of my concern for Japheth. I asked him to please take me to the family. He informed me that they were staying with the baby in Ward 4 of the hospital. I immediately went there, but they had gone out for a while.

At 2:00 PM I returned to Ward 4, and Japheth was sleeping soundly with an IV in his arm. His mother was using this respite to take a shower. I sat on the edge of the infant's bed as a roach and a spider crawled on the wall near his head. I touched his little feet. They were cool to my touch. However, the upper portion of his body was still very hot.

When his mother returned to his bedside, I explained the rehydration drink to her. Japheth, however, did not have a bottle and was too weak to drink from a cup. I promised her that the first thing in the morning I would go to town and buy a bottle for him. (Thankfully his mother still breast-fed him.)

I asked how long Japheth had been in the hospital. She said, "Off and on for six weeks."

I asked, "How long have they been giving him glucose water via IV?"

She replied, "Just now, this afternoon, for the first time."

I was outraged at this information. One thing I couldn't stand was this hospital's reputation for killing patients instead of healing them.

One good thing I learned from Japheth's mom, however, was that when the couple came back to the hospital after church Sunday morning—they had left the hospital to bring Japheth to Genesis Church to be prayed for—little Japheth smiled and cooed for the first time in over a month. She believed that God had already healed the source of the sickness and that the healing of the diarrhea and vomiting was only a matter of time! I was amazed and encouraged by her faith.

In the afternoon of March 12, I went back to the hospital. In the morning, we had gone to town to buy a bottle, some vitamin drops, and a rattle for Japheth. I now went to give them to him. His mom had been faithfully giving him my "prescribed" rehydration drink with a spoon. She couldn't wait until I got the bottle. Since the day before he had already drank half of a liter.

I asked if he had thrown up at all. She said, "No!"

I touched Japheth and his fever was totally gone. Not only that, I asked her about his urination. She said that it began to be strong again, like a normal baby's, that day. (Before, it was just a trickle and only water.)

I gave Japheth a dose of vitamin drops and showed his mother how to give it and how much to give Japheth each day. A nurse came over in the process and was almost in tears as she thanked me for giving him the vitamin drops and for caring for him the way I did. She explained that the hospital was short of all that kind of thing.

It was my pleasure to care for Japheth. I am so thankful to God for healing him and for giving me wisdom to react to the situation and to do the right thing. I told his mother that we needed to be thankful that we served a great, big God.

"Oh, yes!" she said. "Every morning when I wake up, throughout the day, and when I go to bed at night, I thank the Lord for healing my baby!"

Another good thing that came out of this situation was that Japheth's father told us that he and his wife planned to make our Pentecostal church their home church "because your prayers carry results!"

That is the main reason for miracles: to draw people to the truth of Jesus Christ.

Brian and Esther Henry are alumni of Christian Life College. After his Bible college graduation Brother Henry became the administrator/secretary-treasurer for the United Pentecostal Church of Tacoma, Washington. He served there until he and his wife left for Papua New Guinea in 1994. After serving as associates in missions in Papua New Guinea for almost two years, they received their missionary appointment in January 1996. They are currently the only resident UPCI missionaries in Papua New Guinea. They live in Goroka in the highlands and administer the Bible school. Brother Henry states that they have "a big job on [our] hands in training ministers and building a new Bible school facility."

The Henrys returned to the field after their deputation was completed in August 1998.

Chapter 24

Philippines: He Is More Than Enough for Me!

By Marivic Batacan
Submitted by **David Brott**
Missionary to Asia and Pacific/LDI

My name is Marivic Batacan. I am from Makati City, Philippines, and am the mother of two daughters and a son. Before I met Jesus Christ my Lord, I worked as an entertainer in Japan for five and a half years. Because of that atmosphere, I became a drug user. I took several kinds of drugs, and I also smoked cigarettes often. I felt I had to do these things because of my lifestyle as an entertainer. It was easier for me to make a large sum of money from the customers if I was drunk or high on drugs.

I came back to the Philippines because I had become pregnant. I still had many vices even though I was already pregnant. I played cards and gambled several hours every other day. I spent all the money I had saved. I had many diseases, such as tuberculosis. Furthermore, a goiter in my neck was getting bigger every day, and I was bleeding because of a tumor.

In 1993 some of my relatives who were already

believers invited me to go to church. I still remember the first time I attended Sunday service at Philippine Evangelism Center, the UPCI headquarters church. As I stood at the door and heard the congregation singing, tears started to stream from my eyes, and I felt gladness in my heart. I went to the altar and lifted my hands. As I cried aloud, saying, "God, please forgive me for all my sins," I felt something moving inside my body—from my throat, down to my stomach, then to my knees. I knew that God healed me that moment. The next Sunday I was baptized in water in Jesus' name, and now I'm totally healed. Our God is so wonderful!

He's showed me over and over that He's the greatest healer. He healed my elder daughter, who had skin allergies from birth until she was twelve years old. She used to stay longer at the hospital than at home. She took daily injections of medicines and was not allowed to eat shrimp and oily foods or to use perfume, powder, or lotions. Yet, her condition became worse every day. But our God, Jehovah-Rapha, moved in His compassion and power to heal my daughter through our faith, fasting, and overnight prayer.

He also healed my son, who was an epileptic and asthmatic. My son would have frequent seizures. He would collapse, his body would become rigid, and he would have difficulty breathing. But we still placed our trust in God, and we believed that nothing was impossible for God if we believed in His name. So as I served the Lord Jesus Christ with all my heart, soul, mind, and strength, He touched my son and healed him completely!

The greatest gift that God has given me was that my younger daughter was born completely healthy. While I was pregnant, I had not taken vitamins, drunk milk, or eaten good vegetables and fresh fruit. Also, I had been bound with many vices, so I prayed to God. I said that if He would give me this child, normal and healthy, I would serve Him as long as I lived. He has never failed me. Whatever I asked of Him, I knew He would do it, because God is not slack concerning His promises. God gave me a healthy and talented baby girl. Thanks be to God. He is more than enough for me!

Presently, I am the Sunday school director in a United Pentecostal Church, and my elder daughter is the youth president. We are both very involved in the music ministry of the church. Since we began serving the Lord, we haven't had to go to the hospital or to take any medicines. Jesus healed us mentally, physically, and spiritually. Praise the Lord!

David Brott, a graduate of Conquerors Bible College, and his wife, Kathy, received their first appointment as UPCI missionaries to the Philippines in May 1983. Brother Brott served as the Metro Manila evangelism coordinator and president of Apostolic Center for Theological Studies. After a term of service, the Brotts returned to America. He pastored Bethel Christian UPC in Omaha, Nebraska, served on the district board for over eight years, directed ministers training seminars for the district, and founded L-TAP Regional Ministries, a leadership training program.

In January 1996 the Brotts were reappointed as missionaries to the Philippines and the Pacific and Asia Regions. While Brother Brott's ministry centers on ministerial training and leadership development throughout the two regions, he is also involved in leadership training for the Foreign Missions Division.

Chapter 25

Philippines: As He Said, "Jesus!"

By **Cecil Sullivan**
Missionary to the Philippines

The Philippines is experiencing a great move of the Holy Ghost. In 1998-99 alone we had almost nine thousand people receive the gift of the Holy Ghost. Many of these I witnessed myself as I have traveled throughout the islands, teaching seminars, holding crusades, and accompanying several Dream Team crusades. We are pushing into new areas where the gospel has never yet been preached. This magnitude of revival takes prayer, preparation, organization, and much work. It also has much opposition.

One such case concerns Pastor Eulogio Marinas from Lultan, Dimataling, Zamboanga Del Sur. He is the pastor of our United Pentecostal Church in that area. The church is located in a strong Muslim area. During the past several years, Muslims have killed several denominational pastors and have even harassed and assaulted entire congregations.

Pastor Marinas has recently been having a great move of God and has converted several Muslims. For this reason, the Muslim leaders in the area hate him and have threatened him several times.

Things became deadly serious on the evening of

Pastor Eulogio Marinas

July 10, 1998. Pastor Marinas was sitting in front of his church when a troubled young man walked up to him and, at a distance of six feet, pointed a .357 Magnum pistol at his face. Startled, Pastor Marinas jumped up and said, "Jesus," at the precise moment that the man pulled the trigger. When Pastor Marinas said, "Jesus," he supernaturally caught the bullet in his teeth! Unbelievable? Only by the mighty hand of God do we experience phenomena such as this.

The gunman fired again. The bullet hit Brother Marinas in the upper left shoulder, but it miraculously bounced off, leaving only a bruise. It broke the skin and drew blood, but it did not penetrate the flesh. The man fired a third time at point blank range, hitting Brother Marinas in the upper right shoulder. Again the bullet did not penetrate the flesh but fell to the ground after striking him.

Shots four and five misfired, giving Brother Marinas the essential few seconds that he needed to reach out and twist the pistol from the man's hand. Neighbors who had heard the shots grabbed the assailant and dragged him to the police.

After three days, Brother Marinas decided to go to the jail and talk to the young man. He explained to him, "I know you have a family, and if I file charges, you will be put in prison for a long time. If this happens your family will suffer. Your children will suffer. To show that I do not have any bad intent against you, I am dropping the charges so that you can return to your family."

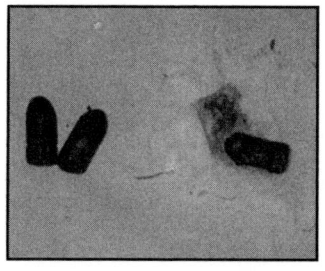

I have a copy of the hospital's medical-legal certificate verifying the gunshot wounds to Brother Marinas's gum, lip, and left shoulder. I also have pictures of the blood-covered bullets that are in our headquarters office under the care of our national superintendent, Romy Navallo.

Without a doubt, "The name of the LORD is a strong tower: the righteous runneth into it, and is safe" (Proverbs 18:10).

Burdened for missions for many years, Cecil and Carolyn Sullivan received their appointment to the Philippines in 1987. Brother Sullivan first came into contact with the Filipino people while in the U.S. Navy in the 1960s. Two years after receiving the Holy Ghost in 1969, the Sullivans began pastoring the Fountain of Life Tabernacle in Zeigler, Illinois. They pastored there for seventeen years and also founded the Zeigler Christian Academy.

The Sullivans spent their first term in the Philippines teaching and establishing twenty new churches in the remote Bicol region. As president and teachers at Apostolic Center for Theological Studies (ACTS) in Manila, they ministered to and taught eighty students to be "revolutionaries for Jesus" during their second term. Now in their third term, the Sullivans continue their training ministry.

Chapter 26

Singapore: Sister Jocelyn and Silkair Flight MI 185

By **Steve Willoughby**
Missionary to Singapore

You hope it never happens, but it did. The headlines splashed the horrific news across the front page: "Silkair Flight MI 185 Lost Over Indonesia."

On the evening of December 19, 1997, a Silkair jet with 104 passengers aboard fell with such force that it literally buried itself in the murky depths at the mouth of the Muri River off the coast of Indonesia's Kalimantan Island. What started as a two-hour routine flight from Jakarta to Singapore ended in Singapore's first air disaster. No one survived.

As the shocking news spread, families of victims stood in staring unbelief. The somber mood spread across the entire tiny island nation. People from every walk of life paused to mourn and to say prayers. A public national funeral was conducted. Condolence books were put out at a memorial field with thousands of people coming to show respect for the dead by signing their names and leaving flowers. Yet in the midst of all the sorrow, one family celebrated.

On December 18, 1997, the doorbell rang on an uneventful day. Sister Jocelyn Velasco went to the gate to collect the envelope from the courier, as she had done dozens of times before. She signed for the envelope, knowing that airline tickets for her employer's son were inside.

Sister Jocelyn works as a housekeeper for an elderly Chinese woman. The employer's unmarried son also lives in the house. His job keeps him in the air flying throughout Southeast Asia two or three times a week. It was cleaning as usual until the tickets arrived. From the moment the tickets were put in Sister Jocelyn's hand, she had an unexplainable fear. Walking back to the house, a kind of dread came over her. It was strange to be feeling this way. In fact her major emotion for the past few months had not been fear but joy. Sister Jocelyn was a new convert.

It had only been six months—but what a joyous six months it had been—since Sister Jocelyn had received the Holy Ghost. During that time she had learned the value of listening to the voice of God. More than anything else she wanted God to use her to be a blessing to others.

But what was this fear? Could it be from God? She was not sure, but she did not think so—at least not at first. Sister Jocelyn laid the tickets on the hall table and went back to work. However, every time she came near those tickets, she had a foreboding feeling. Finally she prayed, "God, are You trying to tell me something about those tickets?" What God seemed to say was simply, "Those tickets are bad."

That was not much information, and she had a hard time explaining herself. But as the foreboding feeling persisted, she felt that she had no choice but to speak to her employer about the matter. After listening to Jocelyn's story, the employer asked, "What do you think I should do?" Sister Jocelyn said, "I think you should ask your son not to go on this trip." Because the employer had come to respect her housekeeper's new faith the past few months, she persuaded the son not to make the scheduled trip.

The next morning the headlines screamed the chilling story of the fateful crash. Watching the news, the son got a sinking feeling in his stomach. With deliberate steps he went to the hall table where the tickets were still laying. Carefully he pulled the tickets from their paper tomb; joy and fear and relief and terror shook his body. Staring at him was the seat reservation on MI 185. Except for a Filipino maid who had determined to be led by the Spirit, he would have been on the doomed flight. With shaking hands and a trembling voice he told the story to his mother. She burst into tears of gratefulness, and they wept together.

They brought Sister Jocelyn in and told her the story. The mother knew that to say "thank you" was not enough. She instructed the son to return the ticket for its cash value. They then gave the money to Sister Jocelyn as a bonus. The mother next called for a family gathering and had a banquet. Sister Jocelyn was made the guest of honor and given credit for saving the young man's life. Sister Jocelyn said, "Oh no, it was not me. It was Jesus whom I serve!"

Steve and Barbara Willoughby received their missionary appointment to Malaysia and Singapore in October 1986. Brother Willoughby wrote: "Our appointment was a dream come true after fifteen years of various mission involvements. While I was a teen, visiting missionaries made a tremendous impact on my life. I was a youth leader of a great group of teenagers who loved working for Sheaves for Christ, and it was foreign missions that motivated us."

Following their trip to the 1984 World Conference in

Manila, the Willoughbys served as associates in missions furlough replacements in Pakistan for the George Shalms. After receiving their missionary appointment and completing deputational travel, the Willoughbys lived in Kuala Lumpur, Malaysia, until God miraculously provided resident visas so they could live in Singapore. The growing Singapore church reflects the Willoughbys' joy, sincerity, and evangelistic zeal.

The Willoughbys returned to the field following a short furlough in October 1998.

Chapter 27

Argentina: I Still Know the Peace Speaker

By **Kay Burgess**
Missionary to Argentina

"Please, senora, come with me. Nothing will happen."

I whirled around. The softly spoken words did not fit the occasion. I found myself staring into the barrel of a pistol as an armed man roughly jerked me out of the door of the vehicle to which I was trying to secure "the Club" against theft. As he pushed me over to where my husband was standing at the gate of our carport, I realized with a shock that my husband was also being held at gunpoint, along with a national pastor and a young man who had been working in our home. Although it felt like a dream, as if I were watching the scene from a distance, what was happening was very real. The three armed men were in earnest as they herded us all back into the garage. They then closed the door behind themselves and began to ransack the house and to remove everything of value that they could carry.

They made the three of us sit on the floor of the garage, guarded by one waving a pistol in our faces, as the other two men took my husband alone through the house searching for money. I sat in mute terror and frustration, as I watched nothing happen. Nothing to him was the violation and destruction of the sanctity of our home—the refuge we work so hard to protect while serving God in a foreign country. Although we had felt the sting of casual theft before—snatching a purse or wallet on the street or breaking into a vehicle—to be accosted in our home while trying to lock up for the night was a nightmare almost beyond belief.

The pastor and his helper had been working extremely late, trying to correct a plumbing problem that developed during a remodeling project in our home. The bathroom and kitchen were totally stripped and gutted—the out-of-date plumbing system completely ripped out of the concrete walls. We had endured being without running water for two days, knowing that the end product would be worth it. Now, however, we had to watch the money we had saved for the project walk out the door in the hands of the armed thieves.

I had obtained the money that morning as my husband stayed with the workers, trying to get our home livable again. When I returned to the house, I had placed the cash in a drawer, not wanting to leave it in my purse during the day. I quickly went to work and forgot about it. My husband did not even know where the money was or that it was in two separate bundles.

Once the thieves found money in the house and realized that we were foreigners, they were convinced we were hiding much more and threatened to kill my son and me if we did not give it to them. They herded the two nationals and me from one room to another with a gun in my back—the man guarding us wanted to be in on the action.

My assailant followed me into my son's bedroom, and I watched in horror as he waved a gun in the face of my son, Kameron. The thief took Kameron's Super Nintendo and all the games he had been playing with just before going to bed. He took my child's coats and other clothing off the pegs, intending to steal them also, but he was unable to find anything to carry them in.

The loss of things that you value can be painful to your wallet. But the humility and indignity of watching your personal belongings displayed before strangers goes even deeper. And the frustration of watching a father assaulted and humiliated, trying to protect the life of his family, is a pain almost beyond description, especially knowing that mentally and physically he was superior to them. Yet the knowledge that one false move could result in tragedy rendered him powerless.

In looking back, I find it ironic that they were smart enough to find all the cash and sellable items but took an old iron that had been spitting rusty water on my clothes while leaving a 2,500-dollar keyboard in the case, ready to go. They could not steal the stereo because it was in the shop. Nevertheless, they took all of our CDs anyway, not taking time to notice that they were all in English and all gospel.

As one of the intruders held a gun to my husband's head and demanded money, he received a call on his cell phone. Evidently the caller asked what he was doing, because he replied, "I'm working." They left fingerprints all over the house, but they were smeared and useless because they were so nervous, high on drugs, dirty, or all of the above.

You wonder where God was in all of this? Oh, He was there all right. He was there helping us to keep our wits and not to do anything stupid. He was there in restraining three nervous trigger fingers and in limiting the physical damage to our ransacked house, empty wallets, and my husband's sore jaw. He was there in protecting an impressionable five-year-old, who never really did understand what was happening although he witnessed it all. And He was there, His name on my lips, as I remembered His voice telling me just three weeks earlier that we would have experiences like never before, yet we would still see revival that we could not even begin to imagine.

Without warning a few days after the robbery, I found myself remembering this drama and having some very real panic attacks. I felt that the peace of our home had been violated, and I wanted to do something to change the atmosphere. After we had prayed and I had calmed down a little, I went looking for some good music to fill the house. I found a well-worn cassette and stuck it in an old player that the thieves did not consider worth stealing.

The first words I heard were, "I know the Peace Speaker. I know Him by name." I sat on the floor and listened to the song twice, while crying and thanking God for reminding me that my peace comes from Him!

I could actually feel His peace flow through my heart and back into my home. How good it is to feel the peace of knowing that you are in the absolute will of God and that He is with you in whatever valley you may walk through! Although I feel shaky, very fragile, and somewhat vulnerable at times, I know that God is in control and that He is still the Peace Speaker.

Ken and Kay Burgess went to South America in 1989 to serve as associates in missions in Paraguay and Argentina. This was in response to a missionary call that Brother Burgess experienced when he was sixteen years old. While an AIMer in Paraguay, Brother Burgess was the national youth president, an assistant to the superintendent, and a Bible school instructor. In Argentina, he oversaw the day-to-day operations of the Bible school.

Brother and Sister Burgess received their full missionary

appointment in October 1991. Concerning his work in Argentina, he states, "I am the president of the Bible school, the director of our home missions fund-raiser, coordinator of the national conference, advisor to the youth department, and in charge of the promotion and publication of all literature."

Having completed their furlough, the Burgesses returned to the field in July 1998.

Chapter 28

Chile: The Accident That Did Not Happen

By **Roy Well**
Missionary to Chile

After leaving the continent of South America, I took a half-hour ride on a commercial ferry across a section of the Pacific Ocean to the large Chilean island of Chiloe. I was alone and headed home, twenty-two hours away, after visiting our island churches. Nearing the northernmost city on the island, I was driving on the main thoroughfare. As I had the right-of-way, I was unconcerned to see a car nearing the intersection, coming from the direction of Ancud to my left. The driver, however, did not see me. As is very common in Chile, a stop sign really doesn't mean stop. Therefore, the other car did not stop.

Without a berm to use, I immediately applied the brakes and began to slide on the dry pavement. To my right, where normally there would have been a place to move over to avoid an accident, was a steep bank and a bay of the Pacific Ocean. There was no way to avoid the accident!

The car that had run the stop sign was now so close that I could not see his front bumper. Even with my seat belt on, a crash in the side of our Sheaves for Christ car would have been fatal because of the speed that both cars were traveling.

What happened next, I cannot explain. It seems that for a time I simply did not exist. It was as though God had turned off the lights! The next thing I remember is that I was nearing the bridge across the bay of the Pacific. There had been no accident.

The car that was going to hit me was about thirty-five yards ahead of me, and I was driving peacefully as if nothing had happened. After we crossed the bridge, I stopped the other car to see if the driver could tell me what had happened.

As I walked over to him, he was visibly shaken. He said, "Sir, I don't know what happened back there, but if I did any damage to your car, I will pay for it all."

I suppose I will never know just what happened, but it seems as if God lifted me out of the way of danger. To God be the glory!

After graduating from Apostolic Bible Institute in 1961 and ministering for sixteen years in the United States, Roy and Beverly Well received their missionary appointment in 1977. They worked for over a year in Venezuela, but being unable to obtain permanent resident visas, they transferred to Chile.

Brother Well superintends the UPC of Chile. Sister Well is the ladies president. They both teach in the Bible institute and are thankful that the church has experienced consistent growth under their leadership. Many students have graduated from the Bible institute and are involved in ministry.

In a country that is as long as the United States is wide, missions work is a real challenge. The Wells have helped to establish churches from the most northern city of Arica to the frigid Straits of Magellan, covering 2,600 miles.

Chapter 29

Ecuador: Sacrificial Giving—A Pathway to God's Blessings

By **Stuart Lassetter**
Missionary to Ecuador

The Central Church in Quito had been blessed and, after attendance had consistently run over six hundred for a while, had decided to remodel the sanctuary to accommodate more people. The work would be expensive and would have to be completed during Ecuador's worst economic problems of seventy years. But by faith the pastor presented the need to the church and the plan to remodel.

The need for finances for the remodeling was great, and the pastor announced to the church that on the first Sunday of 2000, a special offering would be received. But the offering would not be for the remodeling! It would be for a national offering to buy land for churches that do not have their own land and to meet in rented rooms or in church members' homes. The pastor explained that before taking care of its own needs, he wanted the Quito Central Church to bless someone else by contributing to this offering.

The people came prepared and gave a sacrificial offering equivalent to about three hundred U.S. dollars for the offering to help other congregations. Later on the very same week, a church member came with this report.

She was from another United Pentecostal Church in a different city and had been in a Quito Central service some weeks before when the pastor announced the need to enlarge the sanctuary. God moved her in that service to give an offering toward the need, but she didn't tell anyone. Now she had gotten the money and had come to give her offering. It was six hundred dollars, twice as much as what the church had given in the offering!

Another week or two went by and unexpectedly the pastor received a phone call from some Ecuadorians who now live in Europe. They were members of the Quito Central Church before they moved away. They desired to send a special offering. When the pastor received the offering it was eight hundred dollars!

This church has been blessed because the pastor and the congregation have learned Bible principles of giving sacrificially to benefit others!

Stuart Lassetter, a former associate professor at Eastern Kentucky University, and his wife, Nancy, were appointed in 1981 to Colombia. During their first term he helped to construct and to establish the Bible school in Cali, served as a Bible school teacher, taught seminars, and preached. She taught in the Bible school and helped train pastor's wives.

The Lassetters transferred to Ecuador in 1986. He is the field superintendent and president of the Bible school and devotes time to pastoral studies, seminars, leadership training, and administrative duties. She works with pastors' wives and the ladies ministry, and is involved in training and seminars.

The Lassetters have completed eighteen years of missionary service and returned to Ecuador in May 1998. Brother Lassetter was recently named the coordinator for the Leadership Development International (LDI) program in South America. In addition to the work in Ecuador, he and Sister Lassetter are involved in teaching LDI seminars.

Chapter 30

Faith Promise Ministries: It Really Does Work!

By **Mervyn D. Miller**
Director of Faith Promise Ministries

Throughout the year, reports flow into the Foreign Missions Division's office concerning miracles that have transpired after someone made a Faith Promise commitment. The following is only two testimonies of many that could be given to show that Faith Promise works. It really does!

The Keith Boydston Family

Keith Boydston attends the United Pentecostal Church of Groves, Texas. He wrote:

"About a year ago, Brother Mervyn Miller came to our church and presented the Faith Promise concept. At that time my family was just making ends meet. We paid our tithes regularly, gave offerings to support the building fund, and donated monthly pledges to Spirit of Freedom and the Tupelo Children's Mansion.

"At the Faith Promise service that night, my wife and I decided to double our monthly commitment to missions and our regular offerings to our local church. My bills and payments had also increased dramatically about this time because one of my children began college. I had the extra expenses of college tuition, books, and a vehicle for my child.

"The Lord blessed, however, and I began to get extra overtime at work, and from that time forward, we always seemed to make just enough to pay my regular bills, my new commitments, and my child's college expenses.

"About six months after making the new commitments, the company that I work for went up for sale. We were one of the largest companies of our kind in America. There was much speculation about what would happen to our company once we were bought out. Finally, after several months, we found out that another company had successfully bought us out. The employees in this new company were making thirty percent less than the employees of equal status at my company. We were expecting a big pay cut. But my wife and I kept paying our commitments, and my wife kept reminding me to trust God.

"Finally after a couple of months of downsizing, in which eight hundred people took an early retirement or were laid off, the new management scheduled a company meeting to explain to all employees what their new roles in the new company would be. That morning my supervisor called me into his office for a discussion. He told me everyone in the company would take a three- to twenty-percent cut in pay. However, a new position had been added due to the restructuring of two combined companies, and my supervisor had recommended me for that position. This new position would increase my pay by at least nine hundred dollars per month if I did not work extra overtime. Also, because of a deal our old company had made right before it was sold, each employee from our old company was to receive a cash settlement to be put into our retirement accounts. The portion that I received was over $117,000.

"To God be the glory! And yes, I will be increasing my Faith Promise in our next commitment service."

The Dane Family

C. Renea Dane of Brownsville, Texas, testified:

"My husband and I took on the twelve missionaries on Foreign Missions Day at the General Conference in Nashville. We own a business called Carissa's Bows. We presently supply 2,223 Wal-Marts with Katy Sue hair bows for children. After returning from conference, I set up appointments with HEB Grocery Company, Brookshire Grocery Company, and Albertson's Grocery Company to sell hair bows to them. God has opened doors with each of these chains. Albertson's Grocery Stores/America Drug Stores are placing a $596,000 order for spring 2000 with us! We do not yet have the totals on sales with HEB Grocery Stores or Brookshire Grocery Stores, but we do know that they have set us up in their computers as vendors and plan to order for spring 2000! We give God the glory for these wonderful blessings.

"We have learned that you cannot outgive God! We would like to immediately take on twelve more missionaries with the goal of supporting all UPCI foreign missionaries."